# Behind The Curtain
-
## The Real Enemy Everyone Is Overlooking

By: Jaime Garza

Cover By: Jarod Garza

All Rights Reserved
Copyright 2025
ISBN: 979-8-9859224-2-4

## DISCLAIMER

This book explores ideas and perspectives that may challenge traditional beliefs, including religious and cultural views. The intent is not to offend, disrespect, or diminish anyone's faith, but rather to encourage critical thinking, open dialogue, and personal reflection.

It dives into controversial, often uncomfortable territory—especially when it comes to religion, tradition, and the stories we've been told to never question. If you're looking for safe, familiar narratives, this probably isn't for you.

Readers are encouraged to approach the content with an open mind and to draw their own conclusions.

The aim isn't to insult or convert—it's to provoke thought. Some of what you read may challenge long-held convictions. That's the point. Truth doesn't fear scrutiny, but dogma often does. If something here rattles you, ask yourself: is it because it's false—or because you were told never to ask?

The views expressed are those of the author and are presented for the sake of exploration and discussion. They are not intended to represent any specific religion, denomination, or organization.

If any part of this book causes discomfort, let it serve as an invitation to examine why—and to seek deeper understanding, whether through agreement or opposition. Take what resonates, question what doesn't, and above all—think for yourself.

## Table of Contents

Foreword..................................................................5
Part I – Introduction..............................................9
Chapter 1 – Who Is Satan..................................12
Chapter 2 – The Slow Fade................................16
Chapter 3 – Strongholds....................................21
Chapter 4 – Giving Place to The Devil............24
Chapter 5 – Symbols..........................................34
Chapter 6 – Generational Curses....................40
Chapter 7 – Counterfeits of Satan..................43
Chapter 8 – The God of This World?..............47
Chapter 9 – The Flesh........................................51
Chapter 10 - The Bible......................................56

Part II – Introduction........................................62
Chapter 11 – The Media....................................64
Chapter 12 – Internet of Things......................71
Chapter 13 – Water ............................................77
Chapter 14 – Pesticides....................................86
Chapter 15 Food..................................................89
Chapter 16 - Endocrine Disruptors................95
Chapter 17 - Chemical Skies .........................101
Chapter 18 - Vaccines......................................111
Chapter 19 – Covid...........................................127
Chapter 20 – The Earth....................................139
Chapter 21 – Aliens..........................................164
Conclusion..........................................................170

## Foreword

We are starting to see the decline of the American Family, as has been the case for some time. The media have propagated a division like never before seen in my lifetime. And lies have been peddled as truth for so long, that even professionals struggle to know what is true and what is false. A whole generation of young adults who are now graduating from high school and university were raised on the backs of technology. TV screens, computer screens, and phone screens became the babysitter, keeping the kids entertained and indoctrinated.

The messaging started out as subtle and subliminal but evolved into a full scale hidden in plain sight type of messages that are now slowly being exposed. At the time, parents didn't know the scale of the messaging that was targeting kids but now stuff is starting to get exposed. Everything from little innuendos in Disney movies to cryptic scenes in music videos, the amount of subliminal messaging geared towards darkness and satanic principles has been steadily increasing.

It's been said that if you control the media, you control the flow of information. And if you control the information, you can control how a person perceives that information. If you can control their perception, then you can control how they feel. And if you control how a person feels about information, then you can control how they will react. And if you can control how they react, then you control them. Once you control them, you can easily guide them in whatever direction you choose. That's how Satan and his pawns have infiltrated and have been operating to control the masses. They've been at it for decades, and maybe even centuries. We are all playing single, double, and triple moves in Checkers, and they're playing long game 3D Chess. It's no wonder that many are still duped into thinking all these connections that are being made and exposed are just coincidences. That's the way it was designed. To keep the masses in-line and destroy any dissent immediately.

They call it the "Tall Poppy Syndrome." Tall Poppy Syndrome is a term used to characterize this field of Poppys, a type of plant that is grown and harvested for its medicinal properties. But the idea is to have all the flowers growing in a way where not one is taller than the others. The goal is to create a uniform height for all the flowers. In essence, the fields look very nice and neat and in order, but it's because any flower that began growing taller than the others was quickly trimmed down to size. That's how dissent and thinking for yourself in this world is treated. They do this in various ways. One way is to have the person labeled as a quack or conspiracy theorist and so any information that is from them is quickly dismissed.

Another way is to place "experts" with opposing viewpoints in front and center and the media just runs with it. And because these are experts, regular people are not smart enough to analyze of think for themselves. Another way is to drown out the opposing viewpoint with so much rhetoric that it gets lost in the sea of information and repetition. And the last way is to just create cognitive dissonance. This is when something is repeated so often, it becomes an indelible fact in the mind of the person who heard it. So when an opposing fact is introduced, it is immediately shut down and the person refuses to see it as factual, no matter how logical or truthful it really is. They have closed themselves off from the possibility that anything that goes against their closely held belief would actually be true. They ignore the evidence that challenges their existing view and will even distort facts that contradict their preconceptions, favoring emotional comfort over objective reality. Even if these beliefs were instilled in their mind through repetition and strategy. Even if there was an overwhelming amount of evidence that contradicted it. Their view would filter out anything that wasn't aligned with what they had already pre-decided, and their truth would stay incontrovertible. That is where we are as a society. And that should scare us all.

# Part I – The Spiritual Side of This Battle

## Part I – Introduction

It's been said that hard times create strong men. And those strong men, in an effort to make it better for those that come after, tend to create good times. The problem is that good times then go on to create weak men. And those weak men indirectly create hard times. That's how the cycle works. As simple as it may seem, many fail to see what this truly entails or how it affects generational blood lines. We have been so blessed that we have taken it all for granted and have lost sight of simple concepts. Modern society has fostered so many conditions that have led to a prevalence of entitlement, diminished self-discipline, and a lack of self-reflection.

The Gospel of Jesus Christ sounds very strange to a generation that has been taught they are perfect just as they are, loving themselves is virtuous, following their heart is the best thing to do, and nothing is more important than being happy. This trend has been shaped by a prioritization of convenience, immediate gratification, and external validation over resilience, introspection, and values. This has contributed to a weakening of personal accountability, emotional fortitude, and spiritual sustenance. Unrealistic expectations about life's challenges has fed into this notion where everyone expects everything to fall perfectly in place, as if by magic. And when things do not, frustration, anxiety, and overwhelm take charge and disorientation takes the helm. Social media has amplified this by promoting curated versions of success, beauty, and happiness, which can leave individuals feeling inadequate or unworthy if they fail to meet these often unattainable standards.

Self-discipline is also another casualty of modern society. The abundance of choices and the reduction of barriers to access have made it easier to indulge in short-term pleasures, which, many times can have long-term consequences. Without discipline, individuals struggle to achieve meaningful goals and struggle to develop a sense of purpose. They lack resilience and have a hard time enduring challenges. And it becomes easier to fall into darkness and away from God. The rationalizing of darkness and evil principles has created a wave where individuals feel they have a right to things that would generally be labeled as wrong or morally corrupt. What God calls adultery, society calls an affair. What God calls it drunkenness, which is a sin, society calls alcoholism, which is a disease. What God calls an abomination and a perversion for a woman to lie with a woman, and a man to lie with a man, society calls it being gay, which means happy. Society today has softened its standards and has allowed sin to be an accepted and common practice so long as it is not called sin. This play on words using euphemisms has degraded culture and has caused things that are wrong to seem okay, or normal. But we must remember that to be accepted by the world, we are actually rejecting God.

These things can easily sway someone into thinking that coincidence runs everything, and in a world filled with chance, there is no God, and there is no Devil. It's just us, here, and now. It's been said that the greatest trick that Satan ever played was to convince the world that he doesn't exist. Because if there is no devil, then there can be no God. And if there is no God, then there's no point in any of this. It's all randomness and coincidences brewing together in a pot of luck and mishaps. There is no rhyme nor reason to any of it. At least that's how they used to want us to think. But we are now living in an age where the Devil doesn't even hide like he used to. Satanism and demonology are now up front and center of many of the things happening around the world. Whether it be in the music industry, the film industry, in professional sports and now even politics, Satan, his demons, and his followers are now openly professing their allegiance through words, actions, outfits, videos, and symbols. And it's all right in front of our faces if we really take the time to look.

# Chapter 1 – Who Is Satan

*"Satan promises the best but pays with the worst; he promises honor and pays with disgrace; he promises pleasure and pays with pain; he promises profit and pays with loss; he promises life and pays with death."* – Thomas Brooks

So who is Satan? In the Bible, Satan is depicted as a powerful spiritual being who opposes God and works to lead humanity astray. The name "Satan" comes from a Hebrew word meaning "adversary" or "accuser," reflecting his role as an opponent to God's purposes. The Bible calls him The Great Deceiver, The Great Divider, and The Great Destroyer. Rev.12:9 states that "The great dragon was hurled down--that ancient serpent called the devil, or Satan, who leads the whole world astray. He was hurled to the earth, and his angels with him. Luke 10:18 says "I saw Satan fall like lightning from heaven." In Revelation 12:7-9, Satan is portrayed as a dragon and the ultimate enemy of God and His people. He leads a cosmic rebellion against God and is cast out of heaven along with a third of the angels. Those angels are what we know to be demons, and Satan is the main dark one.

In 2 Corinthians 4:4 it says Satan, who is the god of this world has blinded the minds of those who don't believe. If you ask most people, they'll say they do believe in God, but then they live, act, and think in ways that contradict that. Their actions, mindset, and even words do not reflect the premise. So it's not so hard for Satan to be deceiving the masses "who don't believe." And this means that because of that, Satan has infiltrated almost every aspect of human life. Everything from medicine to Science to education to politics to entertainment, Satan has stronghold in. And he uses all these avenues to further his agenda. And that agenda boils down to this: separate the people from God and divide the people of God. By keeping people so busy fighting amongst themselves they'll rarely take the time to stop and think, or stop and appreciate, or stop and pray, or stop and love. If Satan can convince us to fight amongst ourselves over topics that were never meant to be up for debate, then he can keep an entire people of God from truly knowing God as a Father. We see this everywhere nowadays due to the media and celebrities sowing seeds of division and separation.

Satan also uses distractions to keep people from their purpose. Distractions can be one of the most subtle yet powerful ways people are kept from realizing or fulfilling their purpose in God. Their energy, attention, and resources are strategically diverted away from what truly matters, often leading to missed opportunities, unachieved goals, and a lack of focus. Frequently giving in to distractions can also create habits of avoidance and indulgence. Juggling distractions often leads to a sense of overwhelm. Constant distractions leave little room for self-reflection or the development of the unique gifts and talents that contribute to one's purpose. This can lead people to chase external validation or artificial goals that aren't aligned with their true self and the purpose that God had planned for them. When one is not living in alignment, it becomes easy for Satan to slip in and sell his lies. And over time, mental and emotional health also begin to suffer.

Satan and his demons also bring temptations into the mix with the goal of keeping people living in sin and separated from the Father. That separation, the space created by the sin tends to expand and grow over time. This can be likened to a boat slowly drifting away from its original anchor point. Without an anchor in place, before long, the distance of that boat to its set point will have become so vast, it would be hard to tell where the anchor would even have been. So then we try looking to God, but because we've drifted so far away, it has become so hard to see or hear Him. We then feel lost and disoriented. So we look for things to distract us. We don't want to look at why we are where we are. We just want to feel better and so we seek comfort.

But in seeking that comfort, complacency fills our life. We become okay with no longer being connected to God. We chalk it up to this idea that we're just doing the best that we can with what we have. But are we really? Satan's plan is to create that separation to God. He's very cunning, and will use human drivers to accomplish that goal. One of those drivers is our need to avoid pain. So when we as individuals seek comfort to avoid pain, we are making space for Satan or his demons to come in and create that disconnection. And even though it may start off slow and unnoticeable, that rift can quickly grow. But because we are comfortable, we don't mind it as much. In that end, Satan has accomplished his goal.

We must learn to see beyond people. The real enemy is lurking in the shadows of the unseen world. In Ephesians 6:12, it states that "our fight is not against the flesh and the blood but rather against the principalities, against powers, against rulers of darkness of this world, against spiritual wickedness in high places." So Satan and his demons do work through people and they do have followers that do his bidding. He does have influence over people that are not connected to God and his influence can manifest in a variety of ways. It's been said that If we don't know our enemy, then we're going to lose every battle we face. Many people are convinced that Satan is not real, or at least, not a real being. And yet we see so many examples of his influence all over the place. But because we don't see it as such and we just assume it's the sign of the times, it becomes easier for Satan and his demons to exert their influence over our lives. This influence may show up as bad habits, sinful thoughts, self-sabotaging behaviors, Anxiety, or even Depression. But one only needs to scratch the surface a bit more to see the root cause of it all. Satan or his demons are making themselves at home in your space and if you don't consciously do something to evict them, it will only get that much harder to do it later on once they've gained a foothold. This is a war against God. And we are right in the middle of it. We must choose a side. We cannot be on the fence because Satan owns the fence. Lukewarm Christianity has no place in the on-going battle because what's at stake is worth so much more than we can imagine. Pick a side, and go all in in that side.

## Chapter 2 – The Slow Fade

*"Sin begins with a single thought. The moment we give place to that thought, we give place to the devil."* -Watchman Nee

There's been a slow gradual fade to where we are now as a society. Stuff that used to be esoteric and hidden in plain sight is now openly proclaimed and glorified. What used to be villainized has now become glamorized. And to the undiscerning eye, it's easy to be swept away in this lifestyle of "do what thou wilt" which basically means do what feels good. They want you to believe that life is short and you should enjoy every ounce of it because you only live once. That kind of thinking has many Christians living in lukewarmness, and Revelation 3:15-16 says "I know your works: you are neither cold nor hot. Would that you were either cold or hot! So, because you are lukewarm, and neither hot nor cold, I will spit you out of my mouth." We must keep in mind what 1 John 2:15-16 says, "Do not love the world nor the things in the world. If anyone loves the world, the love of the Father is not in him. For all that is in the world, the desires of the flesh and the desires of the eyes and pride of life are not from the Father but are from the world." We do this because yes, life is short, but we must remember that eternity happens to be very long. And the way we live here determines where we'll live after, Heaven or Hell.

There is a fine line between light and darkness and Christians today are dancing along that line, merrily going back and forth from light to dark and back to light. That's exactly what Satan and his demons want. They want us living in that middle ground. They want us unaware of what that middle ground truly means, and they want us so immersed in our lives and ourselves that we don't realize the danger that is there. The middle ground is the new battle front. It's where the world is being fought for and it's where Satan does most of his work. Ephesians 4:21 says "Don't give place to the devil." Because once he has a foothold in on your life, even if it's by accident, it opens you up for so much more muddiness. In that muddiness, you confine yourself more and more to that middle ground and the perpetual cycle of sin and separation can quickly develop.

It's easy to fall for Satan's traps because he clothes himself in the things of this world. In art, clothes, music, movies, scholars, leaders, and even heroes. 2 Cor. 11:14 says "And no wonder, for Satan himself masquerades as an angel of light" meaning he can capitalize on our inclination toward light as a way to deceive us.

We do see Satan and his demons daily but not in the form we think, and so we don't give it much thought. But when we sit back and act like he doesn't exist or become indifferent to him and all of his deceptions, then we've already lost. We already fell for the trap and have become victims in this spiritual war that has been going on for quite some time.

Back in the day, life was viewed more as a battleground. It was seen as a constant struggle to avoid hell, and live in such a way to go to heaven. The governing belief was to "Live right, in order to die right, so that you could live again in Heaven." Our grandparents and great grandparents spent most of their days reading their Bible and in prayer. Today it seems like the complete opposite.

Life and everything that comes with it is seen as a playground rather than a battleground. Instead of viewing Earth as a foreign land, we've made ourselves very much at home here. We have lost sight of the fact that we're in a war and our real enemy is prowling around like a stealth lion looking for ways to win souls for his kingdom. Instead of priming and preparing for battle, we are dancing with the devil and rolling around with sin. Instead of fighting, we are frolicking. Instead of preparing for this spiritual war, we are closing our eyes to it, acting like it's not real. We are living according to our fleshly desires and then rationalizing our behaviors with "new age" tolerant beliefs. We may not be murdering, resorting to violence, or even committing adultery, but in the eyes of God, sin is sin. And the muddiness that comes from that sin can keep us in that middle ground where Satan wants us.

It's been said that the difference between a lamb and a pig is, when the lamb falls in mud, it quickly wants to get out. The pig, however, wants to stay in that mud and can wallow in it for as long as it'll be allowed to. It's very much at home in that dirtiness. So that begs the question, are we more like the pig or the lamb right now in this part of our life. Because this middle ground is not where safety and salvation can easily be found.

It's not enough to just watch short clips of a sermon and consider them to be adequate alternatives and good substitutions that can make our crooked paths straight. We cannot just post bible quotes on social media and expect our dirtiness to wash off. We must deliberately cut sin out of our lives and live in accordance with how the Bible instructs us to. Indifference can no longer be an option. Satan depends on our indifference, and our ignorance in order to infiltrate our lives. The smallest crack or opening and Satan or his demonic forces will slither their way in and establish a homestead in our lives.

I used to leave my garage door slightly open to allow it to air out as I exercised in there. There'd even be times when I'd leave it open overnight by accident and in the morning I was so thankful that everything was where I left it. I was worried that someone would break in and steal my stuff. I didn't know that what I should've been worried about was not some other human trying to steal from me but rather rodents that would use my garage as their new resting and breeding ground. So, this "invisible to me" enemy that I never saw was leaving evidence of its existence inside my garage. There'd be rat droppings all over the place, boxes that were chewed up, and smells that only rats could make.

Eventually those rats became so brazen that they began showing themselves with no fear, which in turn actually started causing fear within me. I had to make a decision to set up a bunch of different types of traps and use all types of means to rid my garage of this infestation. That's the way it is with these spiritual things. We open up doorways into our lives either on purpose or unknowingly by accident. In the beginning, it may not be so obvious that something has snuck in. Over time however, evidence will begin to emerge, but to the undiscerning eye, it's just Anxiety, or Depression, or bad dreams, or intrusive thoughts, or just bad luck. Anything in the physical that can be attributed as the likely culprit will be given that credit and anything in the spiritual is quickly dismissed. Eventually however, it will get to a point where these demons become so brazen that they no longer hide nor mask themselves. They will flat out let you know of their presence, and at that point, it can become scary and harder to deal with. The idea is to never let it get so far. But in the end, they all cower before the One True God and the King of Kings.

## Chapter 3 - Strongholds

*"A stronghold is an entrenched pattern of thinking that is contrary to the Word of God. It's a lie the devil has convinced you to believe is true."* Tony Evans

In Scripture, a *stronghold* is often seen as a fortified place, something heavily protected, and nearly impenetrable. While strongholds can be positive when referring to God as our refuge like Psalm 18:2 states, they are more often referenced in the New Testament as something more sinister. In 2 Corinthians 10:4–5, Paul writes that "the weapons of our warfare are not carnal but mighty in God for pulling down strongholds, casting down arguments and every high thing that exalts itself against the knowledge of God." These strongholds aren't always physical. They can be spiritual, emotional, and mental barriers that keep people stuck in cycles of addiction, anxiety, depression, self-sabotage, deception and sin.

Strongholds are areas in our lives where the enemy has subtly, over time, built a structure of lies, brick by brick. Some strongholds often start with a wound, something unresolved or painful. And instead of seeking healing, the enemy whispers that escape is the only viable answer. Over time, a pattern forms, and what started as a temporary fix has become a prison. That thing we once did to help relieve the symptoms now has become a crutch that keeps us stuck.

Other strongholds can be fed by the lie that we are worthless, unloved, or beyond help. Suicidal thoughts are often the devastating endgame of a stronghold that tells someone they have no hope, no future, and no value. These are lies that directly contradict God's Word. But because we haven't been filling our cup with the word of God, we become hypnotized by the lies of this world. 2 Corinthians 10:5 tells us to "...take captive every thought to make it obedient to Christ." This means that any thought we don't take captive to the obedience of Jesus Christ will make us a captive to Christ's enemy. Satan and his demons attack the mind, and we have to know how to oppose these assaults.

It's been said that a stronghold is a Satanically fortified open door. It's where Satan takes authority when you grant him access. The fact that the door is open is how Satan gains access, but the stronghold is how Satan builds stronger in-roads when you keep allowing him access. In other words, when you don't do anything to close the door, the more time you give him with an open door, the more he builds more fortified strongholds. And he's not just protecting the door, but he's trying to fill in all the spaces behind the door. In doing that, the stronghold becomes harder to eradicate and overcome.

Other types of strongholds are created by the dabbling of dark, occultic things, and the consistent behaviors aligned with sin. When we keep giving permission to Satan, whether consciously or subconsciously, we help build and fortify strongholds. It's important to have the self-awareness to see how we are contributing to these things that keep us stuck. Because the last thing we want to do is to keep doing the same thing and be confused as to why we are not getting different results.

The tragedy of strongholds is that they often feel like truth, especially in the moment. The thoughts and emotions they bring seem so real, so powerful, and so ingrained, that it becomes hard to distinguish them from who we really are and what those strongholds are telling us. But God's Word brings clarity and power. It shines a light into dark places and exposes the enemy's schemes for what they are. The truth is, in Christ, we are not powerless. We are equipped with spiritual weapons, like prayer, Scripture, worship, and the authority of the Holy Spirit. We can use these to tear down these strongholds and reclaim territory in our minds and hearts that belong to God.

Transformation, however, doesn't always happen overnight. But as we renew our minds with the truth as Romans 12:2 tells us, the walls begin to fall, and strongholds begin to lose their grip. So even though strongholds may feel immovable, they are not stronger than the One who sets captives free. Healing is possible and freedom is real. And every lie that has kept us in bondage can be shattered by the truth of who we are in Christ. But we have to be consistent in our walk and live consistent with biblical truth. Only then will strongholds lose their grip and we'll be able to regain our sovereignty under God the Father.

## Chapter 4 – Giving Place to The Devil

*"If you give the devil a ride, he'll want to drive."* -Dwight L. Moody

The presence of an evil entity is something usually shown in horror films, but the truth is, demons do exist. We are trained to believe that there is only this reality that is governed by what we can see, hear, and touch. Anything beyond these things is not considered real but rather a figment of our imagination. However, just looking at how our eyes are built to detect wavelengths of light from about 380 to 750 nanometers, we are very limited to what we can actually see.

We are able to see reds, oranges, yellows, greens, blues, and violets. But beyond that range lies a world we cannot perceive. Infrared light, which is a color of light just beyond red, and ultraviolet light, which is just beyond violet, are completely invisible to us. But not to every organism. Birds, cats, and even dogs, among many other types of animals, are able to see way beyond what we can see. We are limited in what we are actually able to see. So to say that the only things that exist are what we can physically see with our own eyes is completely false. And a part of us knows this.

We see examples when we get a glimpse of something or see things with the corner of our eyes. But every time we look again or take a second glance, there's nothing there. We just assume it's our eyes playing tricks on us and shrug it off. Something may have really been there and our higher senses picked up on it. But we dismiss it because we couldn't fully perceive this other dimension of reality. And because we have been taught and trained to believe in God, but only at a surface level, we believe the spirit realm is not real and our minds are always playing tricks on us. But demons are real, just as is Satan. And if allowed to enter into our lives because we took for granted this other dimension or doors we left open, these entities can quickly attract others and eventually their brazenness cannot be ignored.

There are many different ways that people give place to the devil in their lives. The obvious comes from dabbling in sin. There are other ways that may not be so obvious. For example, our thought choices can steer us toward the light or to the dark. None of us can really control what thoughts enter our minds, but we can control which ones we focus on, linger upon, and bathe in. Our brains can be likened to a filing cabinet with all types of things we've read, watched, or listened to over the days, weeks, months, and years. At times, whether because of a scent, sound, or a memory that was triggered, our brains will subconsciously retrieve one of those files and replay it as you go about things.

Not all those files are good or of God. They may have been recorded at a time when you were living in sin or dabbling with darkness. So, the stuff our brains reactively turn to may not always be keeping us focused on the light. That is why it's important to fill up those filing cabinets with the scripture and anything that is light-centered and Biblical. Philippians 4:8 says, "Whatever is true, whatever is noble, whatever is right, whatever is pure, whatever is lovely, whatever is admirable—if anything is excellent or praiseworthy—think on such things." That's how we consciously fill those filing cabinets so that when our brains reactively want to retrieve something, it can be centered more around noble, worthy, and praiseworthy things.

The harboring of sin is another way that Christians give place for the devil in their lives. Carnal living, which means living for the flesh and all the desires that the flesh wants, can have a short-term effect of pleasure. And one of the human conditions is that we all want to avoid pain and gain pleasure. But having a long-term perspective is what Christianity is about. It's about choosing what we want most over what we want now. In today's culture, this is not a popular concept but an important one if we really want to win this war. It's all about playing "Chess" as long-game while everyone else out here is playing "Checkers" as a short-game. That's how we must see things in order to overcome any tool, strategy, or influence that Satan wants to use against us. That's how we get the upper hand. That's how we inherit the Kingdom of God.

Another way that Christians give place to the devil is in the dabbling of dark and Occult practices. Things that pop culture at one time or another has embraced such as playing with Tarot Cards, getting your palms read, seeing a psychic, and even playing with Ouija Boards. All these things open up a spiritual door for evil to enter. Sometimes this evil masquerades as a family member that has passed, as is the case with Psychic readings and Ouija Boards. It may even know things that only a family member or a close loved one may have known. But it must be made clear, these are not deceased family members. These are disembodied spirits and demons that have access to information which help them slide into our lives and convince us of their importance. They use trickery and parlor tricks to make their presence known as powerful beings. But at the end of the day, they are cheap theatrics used to disguise their vulnerability to the faith and power that the name of Yeshua (Jesus) innately holds. The main idea however is to avoid this altogether by not seeking nor using any of these things that open up these doorways. Because once doorways are opened, it can quickly become free for all.

Amulets, talismans, jewelry, and even outfits that have this "All-Seeing Eye" also known as the Evil Eye or the Eye of Horus have become a popular mainstay in today's culture. This "Eye" made popular by Illuminati Symbology has grown in popularity and now people, not knowing what it really stands for, seek it out as a fashion statement. On the surface, it is something that may seem cool and trendy but it's really just glorifying demonic principles. A beacon of sort, that calls out to other demons to bring about their influence into our lives.

The Goat used to be among the more prominent symbols associated with satanism. However, in today's society, GOAT now stands for "the Greatest of All Time" and to think otherwise is absurd, according to society. In the Bible, goats are associated with separation from God, as seen in the parable of the sheep and the goats in Matthew 25:31-46. The goats symbolize those who did not follow God's will. The lamb often represents purity, innocence, and sacrifice, epitomized by Jesus Christ, who is referred to as the "Lamb of God" in John 1:29. Together, these animals reflect themes of judgment, redemption, and the choice between righteousness and disobedience. The goat is also seen in the Baphomet, which is a famous occult statue/image of a demon which many believe to be Satan. It's got the head of a goat and the body of a human exhibiting male and female characteristics. It also has the legs and feet of a goat. And a pentagram on its forehead.

The inverted cross and the inverted pentagram all pay homage to Satan and his evil influence. Either knowingly, or unknowingly, these symbols help Satan, or his demons get a stronghold and establish a homestead in one's life. These symbols can come in the form of jewelry, outfits, candles, statues, and even artwork. The idea is to avoid them entirely, even if society has embraced them as a trend.

Praying to statues such as Angel of Death, also called "The Santa Muerte", Buddha, The Virgin Mary, or any of the Saints or Apostles is also a form of sin. I know this one may be controversial to some, but The Bible clearly says in Exodus 20:3 "Thou shalt have no other gods before me." In Exodus 20, God commanded the Israelites not to create any graven images or idols, emphasizing His uniqueness and invisibility to prevent them from worshiping physical objects.

In Deuteronomy 4:15-18, Moses reminds the Israelites that when God spoke to them at Mount Sinai, they didn't see any form or image of Him. God deliberately refrained from revealing a physical form because He wanted them to worship Him alone. He didn't want representations of Him or anything in creation. He was trying to guard them against idolatry. God knew that his essence could not be captured or confined by human-made objects. So, by avoiding images or statues, the Israelites were to maintain a pure, spiritual connection with the unseen God, emphasizing faith over visual representation. Today we have forgotten that.

Music is another way that we easily give place to the devil. The main reason for this is because music doesn't need permission to enter into our head, heart, and soul. Satan has armed music strategically in such a way that it can infect, contaminate, and taint God's people with little effort on their part. Afterall, a catchy beat and sticky lyrics can easily have listeners singing along without realizing what the words really symbolize and mean. The more they listen to the music, the more it becomes like a mantra that continues playing in their heads. Every beat and every lyric is going deep into the subconscious, shaping our thoughts and beliefs without us even realizing it. There are theories that these artists, either knowingly or unknowingly, are using witchcraft to gain access and control of our mind. They're putting spells in the music and using sorcery to establish a foothold in our lives.

It's been said that anything that is said or done in sets of 3 is by design used to penetrate past the head and into the heart. Proverbs 4:23 warns us to "Keep your heart with all vigilance, for from it flow the springs of life." Things that are said in a melodic tone with a cadence, over and over, become mantras. And mantras are powerful because they can shape our thoughts and beliefs thus reinforcing patterns in the subconscious mind. The chorus is the hook and that's what it does; it hooks us in. They are saying the same thing, over and over, and so when we sing along, repeating these things without realizing what we are calling it into our lives. Words from music have a tendency to get into our mind, whether we want them to or not. That's why when we were in grade school, they didn't teach us the ABC's by just saying the letters. They taught us the ABCs with a song. Because they know that music, repetition, and deep memory are deeply and uniquely connected. If you lower the volume on the music and just read the lyrics, you get a more clearer picture of what is really being said. You start seeing the dark and demonic nature in its totality and the anti-God energy that is in the music. You can even ask yourself if you really want to do any of the things that the lyrics are saying. Ask yourself if any true Christian would want to be doing any of these things. Or would it ever be okay with Jesus to do the things that the lyrics are saying?

We cannot constantly fill our minds with demonic music and perverted lyrics and wonder why our life is such a mess or why we can't stop sinning. But we expect to go to church for 1 hour on Sunday hoping the pastor can help with all our issues, difficulties and anxiety. The problem is, we've been listening to the word all week, just not the word of God. We've been listening to preaching all week long, just not the preaching around Biblical principles or led by the Holy Spirit. Once this realization sets in, we can begin navigating more strategically so we avoid the pitfalls that come with what we allow into our headspace.

As believers in Christ, it's important to use discernment about the music we listen to because not all music is from God. There is so much popular music that glorifies sin and the Devil and it is by design. We cannot be living like the devil and claim to have Jesus in our life or proclaim Him to be Lord and Savior. As we listen to music, we must ask ourselves, are we feeding the flesh or are we feeding the spirit? Because we cannot be living for Jesus, while at the same time finding enjoyment in the things he died to set us free from.

Dreamcatchers are another way we give place to Satan. These things are supposedly sacred objects intended to filter dreams, allowing positive ones to pass through while trapping negative ones in their web. Originating from Native American cultures and tied to Native American spirituality, dreamcatchers represent a form of Pagan beliefs that conflict with biblical teachings. Deuteronomy 18:10-12 warns against engaging in practices associated with divination or spiritual traditions outside of God's covenant. Plus Satan could use dreamcatchers as a subtle entry point to deceive Christians by normalizing reliance on objects for spiritual protection or guidance, rather than faith in God alone. The argument might be that trusting a dreamcatcher to influence dreams shifts dependence away from prayer or divine connection and opens the door to superstition or demonic influence.

Throughout history, Satan has cunningly employed other various deceptive practices to divert humanity's focus from God, and in modern times, he has weaponized New Age ideologies to confuse even Christians. Through meditation techniques that emphasize self-enlightenment over divine connection, numerology and astrology that replace biblical trust in God's plan with cosmic predictions, and the use of crystals touted as sources of spiritual power, Satan is subtly trying to shift reliance away from the Creator. Magic and witchcraft, often glamorized in popular culture, further blur the lines between God's truth and occult lies, tempting believers into forbidden realms. Even yoga, while marketed as mere exercise, frequently carries spiritual undertones rooted in pantheistic philosophies that conflict with Christian monotheism. Together, these tools create a seductive web, drowning out God's voice and sowing doubt, noise, and confusion among the faithful. And muddied waters keep Christians disconnected from God, forever seeking and never truly arriving.

There are so many other things that have become accepted and even admonished as a society but may have evil influences attached to them. It's important to remember, we are in this world but we are not of it. The god of this world, Satan has found dubious ways to strategically pervert many of the things that society considers harmless, needed, or justified. And as Isaiah 5:20 says, "Woe to those who call evil good and good evil, who put darkness for light and light for darkness…" Using biblical standards to discern is the starting point we should all be employing, especially with so much at stake.

Spirits and demons are real. And our lifestyle, our behaviors, and even our habits determine whether they have legal permission to oppress our life. The way we go about things determines whether or not we open ourselves up to them. Demons are not just myths or scary stories used to get people to live a better life. They are in fact fallen angels, part of Satan's army. They are the 1/3 of angels that rebelled and were cast down from Heaven. When Satan was cast down, Revelation 12:4 tells us "He wrapped his tail around a third of the stars." So they lost their place in Heaven, they lost their station, but they didn't lose their power. And so now they're seeking access. They're seeking an entrance into the Earth and the only way they can do that is through the life of a human. They need access to a human and will gain access through doors that are opened, left opened, or were never shut due to sin, rebellion, trauma, unforgiveness, pride, or idolatry. Anything that goes against God's order and is left unaddressed is fair game for these demons to use. Ephesians 4:27 warns us not to give the Devil a foothold. That means demons cannot just invade our life. They need to be given a foothold. And so spirits attach themselves to behavior.

When demons gain access to our life, they don't come to play. They come to control. But the good news is that you, as a son or daughter of God, are not powerless against them. You don't have to live in bondage, because Jesus already gave us power over them. But now you have to live in a way that agrees and is congruent with that power that Jesus has given you. The question is, are you guarding your gates or are you unconsciously moving in a way that gives them permission? Are you protecting your mind, your heart, and your soul? Because if demons and spirits are real and they need a doorway to enter, then your lifestyles matters more than you think it does. And it's important that you start paying more attention to it so that you stop giving place to the devil.

## Chapter 5 – Symbols

*"Symbols are the language of the soul, bridging the seen and unseen, revealing truths that words alone cannot capture."* –
Author Unknown

Symbols are the language that Satan and these demonic entities employ through their human counterparts. They do this as a means to influence and drive culture in the direction of their choosing. They use celebrities, musicians, professional athletes and political figures to repeatedly lay out and put forth these symbols because they want us to be entranced. They want these symbols to be repeatedly used in all sorts of arenas so that they are seen as cool, fashionable, popular and trendy. But to the discerning eye, that same symbolism they use to drive culture and flaunt their allegiance will also be the way their downfall occurs, especially when the mass awakening happens.

It's been said that once people learn to read and understand the language of the symbols, a great veil will be lifted and everything will be revealed. Everything from the unassuming "Ok" hand gesture to the covering of one eye in photos, symbols are the way to tell who's in the club and who's not. And by knowing who's in the club, one can discern whether that celebrity really is who they say they are or not. And to tell what god they are referring to any time they speak of him.

When we think of the "OK" hand gesture, we see it as a harmless way of acknowledging that everything is okay.

We don't see much more to it. Until we look into how the fingers and the hand in that position symbolize. It's actually three 6's positioned in such a way that is subtle and unassuming, but yet clear at the same time. The index finger touching the thumb makes the one circle and the 3 extended fingers each make up the lines that extend from the circle to make the 6's. Three sixes, or the number 666, is referred to as the "number of the beast" in the Book of Revelation (Revelation 13:18). They flaunt this symbol either randomly in the air or covering one of their eyes, which is also a symbol in and of itself. There are some that may do this sign unintentionally and don't realize what it stands for. But for the most part, when a superstar athlete or celebrity pose for a photo with this symbol, more than likely they know. They are paying homage to their god and in turn hoping to drive others to the same.

The covering of one eye either using the three 6's symbol or just the hand also has its roots in darkness. It symbolizes an all-seeing eye, often portrayed by the occult symbol as the Eye of Horus, or the Eye of Ra or even the Evil Eye as new age religions have deemed it. At its roots, the idea is that it represents hidden knowledge or hidden power, but really, it just shows allegiance to Satan and what he represents.

The hand covering the mouth and the index finger placed vertically over the lips as to say "shhh" also represents a form of symbolism that relates to secrecy and covertness. Many celebrities and athletes that have "sold their soul" have this vow of secrecy and are popularizing this sign as a means to familiarize the masses and entice them with the mystery and curiosity.

In concerts, rappers tell their audience to put their middle finger up in the air as if it's a way for audience to participate in the music in some way. On the surface, it looks like a harmless gesture where all of the audience has their middle finger pointed at the sky, bobbing up and down to the rhythm of the music. However, one only needs to take a closer look at why they would want hundreds or thousands of people pointing their middle finger up to the sky. Could it be that maybe it's their way of getting the audience involved in saying F—You to God? As silly as it may sound or seem, these satanists really do have an agenda of enmity towards God and will use every opportunity they can to oppose him and bring separation to his people.

The "Rock On" hand gesture which also symbolizes "I Love You" in sign language has its roots in Satanism. There are different variations to this gesture, some with the thumb excluded, and others including the thumb. The underlying symbol however is the "devil horns" and does have the intention of magnifying and glorifying Satan. As far-fetched as it sounds, Satan has been on the Earth for a long time and has found very strategic ways to infiltrate a lot of different aspects of human life. Whether it be making this gesture at a concert, or displaying it as you take pictures, or even waving it in the air at your favorite football game, the roots behind the symbol are in fact demonic in nature. And so when you display it, you really are exalting and giving reverence to Satan, whether you realize it or not. And whether your intention is noble or not, the act in and of itself is enough to diminish God and magnify Satan. Ignorance is not always bliss. We can no longer use the excuse that "we just didn't know." The time to start seeing things for what they are and take a stand against things that are not of God is now. And it starts with seeing these symbols and gestures for what they are and not for what they would like us to think they are.

The lightning bolt symbol has been used so much at a subliminal level that now most people don't even take notice when they see it, even out in the open. They've seen it on their favorite sports drink, in the name of their favorite rock band, used in the name of their favorite YouTuber and even on the side of the head of their favorite boy magician. It's now on kids' jewelry, outfits, cartoons and so many other places. What many people may not know is that this lightning bolt symbol is designed to glorify Satan and his fall, for Luke 10:18 tells us "...I saw Satan fall like lightning from Heaven."

The Freemason symbol of the square and compass, often accompanied by the letter "G," is one of the most recognizable emblems of secret societies. Traditionally, the square represents morality and virtue, while the compass signifies wisdom and self-restraint. Though rooted in Masonic teachings about ethics and personal growth, this symbol has been glamorized in popular culture, frequently appearing in films, videos, and conspiracy theories that depict the Freemasons as a powerful, enigmatic group influencing world events. Maybe in the beginning, the intentions were noble and even somewhat Christian based. But as "initiates" progress through the levels or degrees, the rituals become darker, more occultic, and nefarious. In the end, darkness is what they embody, and Satan is who they serve.

The black and white checkerboard also carries masonic symbolism embedded in it. Usually portrayed as a background image, tiles on the floor, or as an outfit that a celebrity is wearing, the black and white checkerboard squares are supposed to signify the dual nature of existence. But it's also about pushing an agenda that stems around mind control and programming, none of which emphasize Jesus or Biblical teachings.

Egyptian symbology, including the pyramid capstone, the Eye of Horus, and hybrid humans with animal heads, just to name a few are part of a Satan's plan to muddy the waters and drive the one true God out of the picture. Pop culture has embraced these symbols and are seen as trendy with a hint of "New Age" pantheism. But at their core, they blur out God and magnify Satan.

The owl has its roots in this deity called Moloch, who was a Canaanite god mentioned in Leviticus, Jeremiah, and 2 Kings of the Bible. He is often associated with child sacrifice and fire. In modern times, music artists have embraced this symbol of the owl as a means to drive culture in the opposite direction of God, even if they don't know it.

The monarch butterfly has its roots in MK Ultra which was a CIA mind control program that started in the 50's. It involved unethical experiments using LSD, hypnosis, sensory deprivation and psychological manipulation with the goal of controlling behavior, extracting information, and psychological warfare. Music artists have also utilized this symbol as a means to drive culture away from God, but also as a form of subliminal messaging. It's one of those things that if you know, then you know…

Part of the ritual is them showing us these symbols and us accepting them as fashion statements or a part of pop culture. But there's a subtextual occult type of communication happening, and the fact that we partake in it in some way makes us part of the ritual. And because we are part of it, our movements, our reactions, and our acceptances are important.

We only scratched the surface on just a few of the symbols being used but it's important to note that symbols are designed to convey hidden messages, signal allegiance, or assert power within secretive networks. Their goal in using all of these gestures and symbols is to acquaint us with their religion but in a way where it doesn't seem like a religion at all. These celebrities and their handlers feel like they can drive culture towards sin in the most subtle ways and in doing so, can shift the perception around these things so that they become more widely accepted.

The symbols also serve as coded language among insiders. Many of these things may seem like fanatical ideas that can't possibly be true. On the surface, they seem harmless enough and maybe even trendy in the culture. So it's easy to follow along and copy what others are doing, especially if culture has embraced it. But to glorify Satan either knowingly or unknowingly still diminishes God and invites darkness into our lives. By remembering that this place is not our true home or where we came from, we can better remind ourselves that the things of this world may not always be what they appear to be. And they may not always have our best interest as Christians in mind. In knowing this, using discernment is paramount, especially today where everything is so upside down and inside out.

But if we learn to read the language of symbolism, a great veil will be lifted. It is then that their allegiance to darkness becomes so obvious, it cannot be overlooked or ignored.

## Chapter 6 – Generational Curses

*"Generational curses are not just chains of fate, but patterns of pain passed down until someone is brave enough to break them and choose healing over history."* – Author Unknown

Generational Curses are examples where demons have been allowed entry into our lives because of something that a family member did or were exposed to. This idea of generational curses can feel overwhelming, especially when people notice harmful patterns like addiction, poverty, anger, self-sabotage, or broken relationships continuing to show up in their lives. These are just a few of the many ways that these generational curses can manifest, repeating in their families, being passed down from generation to generation.

The Bible acknowledges that the consequences of sin can impact multiple generations. For example, Exodus 34:7 explains that God "visits the iniquity of the fathers on the children and the children's children, to the third and the fourth generation." This doesn't mean God is punishing innocent people for their ancestors' mistakes, but it shows how sin's consequences can ripple through families for generations at a time.

However, the Bible also makes it clear that individuals are not doomed to repeat the sins of their parents. Ezekiel 18:20 says, "The soul who sins shall die. The son shall not bear the guilt of the father, nor the father bear the guilt of the son." This verse emphasizes personal responsibility, meaning each person has the power to choose a different path.

Even more encouraging is the hope found in Jesus Christ. Galatians 3:13 declares, "Christ redeemed us from the curse of the law by becoming a curse for us." This means that through faith in Jesus, believers are no longer bound by past sins or destructive family patterns. God's grace breaks chains, offering freedom and a fresh start. In fact, God's mercy is even more powerful than any curse. Deuteronomy 7:9 reminds us that God keeps His covenant of love to "a thousand generations of those who love Him and keep His commandments." So, while generational struggles are real, they are not stronger than God's love and redemption. Through prayer, faith, and intentional choices, families can begin new legacies of healing, peace, and blessing, breaking free from any generational bondage.

The problem lies in sin. When we continue to live in sin, we give power to the generational curses that plagued our ancestors before us.

Every person's life matters infinitely more than they can imagine, for good or for evil. It's been said that if we don't violently slay the Leviathan of sin in our heart, our mind, and our body, we will feed and nourish it unknowingly. And then what we hand over to our kids will be a bigger and stronger enemy than the one we had to deal with. When we're fighting to break the bondage to sin or addiction, we're not just doing it for ourselves. We're doing it for the generations to come. Because the same is true with generational blessings.

There's no middle ground. We're either going to hand to our children curses or blessings, bondage or freedom, Heaven or Hell. We are fighting for every person that comes after us in the family tree; our progeny. So we need to have a generational vision for the impact that our actions can make. It's no longer feasible to be passive about this. Satan wants us to think hour to hour, day by day, picture to picture, swipe to swipe. But we must be mindful that what we choose to do, every action and thought has a consequence. And like 2 Corinthians 10:5 says, we must take every thought captive and make it obedient to Christ. We must get back to doing things on purpose and with purpose. Because everything we deal with in our lifetime will either become a blessing or a curse for the generations to come.

# Chapter 7 – Counterfeits of Satan

*"The safest road to Hell is the gradual one — the gentle slope, soft underfoot, without sudden turnings, without milestones, without signposts."* C.S. Lewis

The devil will try to mimic the power of the Holy Spirit. In Exodus, Moses delivered the message to Pharoah, "Let God's people go." Pharoah stubbornly demanded a sign from God and that's when Moses instructed Aaron to throw down his staff. Right there the staff transformed into a snake. Despite the powerful display, Pharoah remained unmoved and instructed his magicians to mimic the miracle. And they did just that. However, Aaron's serpent devoured their serpent, proving who had more power on their side. So how are we supposed to know or tell the difference between Holy Spirit power and demonic counterfeits?

Satan's imitations are nowhere near as powerful as God's even though he'd like us to think they are. When writing to the Corinthians about the gifts of the Holy Spirit in 1 Corinthians 12:1-3, Paul wrote "I don't want you to misunderstand this, when you were still pagans, you were led astray and swept away in worshipping speechless idols. So I want you to know that no one speaking by the Spirit of God will curse Jesus. And no one can say Jesus is Lord except by the Holy Spirit." Simply put, demonic power will not glorify Jesus. Demonic power does however, glorify man. It glorifies the flesh, the accomplishments, the abilities and intelligence but Holy Spirit power puts the focus on glorification of God. It recognizes that all that we are, all that we have, and all that's possible is purely because of God. The flesh counts for nothing. Power from the Holy Spirit will always point to Jesus. And 1 John 4:1 tells us "Beloved, do not believe every spirit, but test the spirits to see whether they are from God, for many false prophets have gone out into the world." We must test things according to scripture and biblical standards because Satan is a master at counterfeits.

Hebrews 11:1-3 states "That which is seen does not come from that which has appeared." Not only is this a powerful message about faith, but also gives us some insight about reality. There are 2 realms that form one reality. There is the unseen realm of the spirit and then the realm that we inhabit in the physical. We are one person in two parts. We have a physical body and a spiritual soul.

Our physical body was built for this world and our soul was built to connect with God in the spiritual. And so what we experience as human beings correlates with the reality that God made. And as there are beings that inhabit our physical world, such as other people, there are also beings that inhabit our spiritual world, which are angels and demons. They all started as angels, messengers and ministers. In Revelation 12, it mentions a war in Heaven and Satan decided that he would usurp God. Because of pride, Satan and a third of the angels rebelled against God and were cast out of Heaven.

Since then, he has used every chance he can to get what he feels is retribution against God. And because of his enmity towards God, he inverts everything that is of God. Everything God creates, Satan counterfeits. Everything God builds, Satan breaks. Everything that God has, Satan tries to steal. The third of the angels that fell from Heaven alongside Satan became dark and adopted his enmity towards God. They're still supernatural beings, but they are not equal to God and Satan is not the opposite of God. The opposite of Satan would be Michael the Archangel. Satan cannot be God's opposite because God created him. Satan is a created being and therefore cannot be in the same level as the creator. Satan is not the equivalent of God neither. He cannot be everywhere and know all things like God can. He is not omniscient, omnipresent, and omnipotent. Satan operates within the constraints of created beings. Because of this, he has to go about things in a strategic manner.

Satan and his forces can and do observe human behavior, actions, and speech. Much like anyone who watches and listens carefully, they can deduce patterns, weaknesses, desires, and tendencies. For example, repeated sins or struggles may reveal a vulnerability. Words spoken in frustration, fear, or anger can indicate inner turmoil or doubt. Satan deeply understands human nature. He has witnessed human behavior over millennia and knows common patterns of sin, temptation, and moral failure. He can craft temptations tailored to our weaknesses without needing to "read minds." For example, using pride, greed, or lust to lure people away from God's will is an easy feat for him. Manipulating emotions like fear or anger to cause division and doubt is also easy for Satan or any of his demons to do. They are masters of human nature because they've spent so much time observing and learning from it. That is how they can warp the truth and cause so many Christians to fall into sin and separated from God. They've been at it for a long time and have been trying to perfect the way they do it. In John 8:44, Satan is referred to as the "father of lies." He can use misinformation, half-truths, or twisted versions of the truth to deceive and mislead people. This doesn't require omniscience but rather cunningness and strategy. Planting doubts about God's goodness or promises and convincing people their sins are unforgivable or that God doesn't care is how he and his demons can keep the cycle of unworthiness and self-sabotage in place.

The same way the military has rank and files like a commander in chief, a general, colonel and so on, so to does the demonic realm. Satan and all these other fallen angels are in a rank and file, carrying out their mission to hurt God and defile humanity. So what we're up against is not just this physical war that we fight daily, but there is a war behind that war. And there's so much stuff that happens on that unseen side that affects stuff on the physical side.

The Book Of Daniel speaks of the spiritual war. Daniel was fasting and praying for 21 days for the forgiveness of the people of Israel and for God's mercy. An angel appears to him and explains that the delay was due to a struggle with the "prince of the Persian Kingdom." The angel describes being opposed by this spiritual force until Michael, the archangel, helped him. This prince is likely a spiritual being, a demonic force, who obstructs the angel's mission, illustrating the reality of this spiritual conflict in the unseen realm. This reveals that angels, including Michael, engage in direct spiritual warfare with powerful demonic forces that oppose God's plans. It suggests that the physical realm is influenced by spiritual forces, both good and evil, and that God's purposes are carried out through divine intervention in the heavenly realm. Knowing this, we must be aware that there is so much more happening at a level that we cannot see nor understand. The key is to put our trust in God and live according to the standards he set forth. In doing that, the counterfeits of Satan will never gain a footing in our lives no matter what's happening in that unseen realm.

## Chapter 8 – The God of This World?

*"The greatest trick the Devil ever pulled was convincing the world he didn't exist."* -Charles Baudlaire

The Bible mentions that Satan is the god of this world. So because he is the god of this world, it's important to know that he's been here a very long time and has had strategic opportunities to infiltrate every aspect of our way of life. One of the more decisive ways is through the entertainment industry. Film, music, and media are powerful tools used to influence culture and societal trends and serve as a powerful mechanism for shaping perceptions and values. If in fact Satan has infiltrated these areas, it would be easy for him to subtly inject bits and pieces of himself so that followers of Christ would be more easily tainted or led astray.

Consider this notion that Satan, through access to influential big businesses and elite, is embedding covert messages and symbols within the fabric of popular entertainment. These are not mere artistic freedoms but rather intentional markers. They act like breadcrumbs if you will, hinting at agendas, foreshadowing future events or even just designed to stimulate the flesh and cause temptation.

These narratives and symbols, woven into movies, shows, and music, often go unnoticed by the masses, or dismissed as coincidences or creative quirks. Yet, their presence may serve a deeper purpose. Those orchestrating this operate with a chilling confidence that thrives off our collective ignorance. The subtle unveiling of plans, subliminal messaging designed around glorifying sin, and the foreshadowing of events are at the heart of how they wish to drive culture. That is the essence of their strategy: to hide truth in plain sight and drive people away from God. They broadcast their designs across the cultural landscape, secure in the knowledge that few will piece together the puzzle.

Secret societies, whether fully complicit or blindly following in this interplay with Satan and his demonic forces, advance an agenda that exalts darkness while eroding the presence of God. Like strategists in a grand deception, they invert reality, casting lies as truth and truth as lies. In doing this, they maintain a spiritual veil over the eyes of the masses. And they believe they have this immunity to evade accountability, spiritual or otherwise. They feel they have fulfilled an obligation by disclosing their intentions or including the masses in the ritual. And because they put it out there beforehand, they feel they have absolved themselves of any consequences or karmic retribution.

It's been said that Satan has a plan that has been at play since his fall. If he can't make you bad, he'll make you busy. He will distract you and cause you to focus on all the things that don't really matter in an effort to keep you inattentive to the things that do. He will keep you overspending and in debt to maintain an empty, hollow lifestyle. You'll then feel you have holes in your life you need to be constantly trying to fill them. You'll then be forced to work long hours and even entertain the idea of working 2 jobs just to help make ends meet. You'll be discouraged from spending time with the family, because Satan knows that when homes disintegrate, generational issues and curses are born. He will keep you over-stimulated with smartphones, TV, computers, and internet so that you can't hear God speaking nor have time to read your Bibles. He will keep you chasing material things in hopes that the empty spaces in your life can be supposedly filled.

Satan will put attractive, alluring, and captivating models on covers of magazines and TV to keep you focused on outward appearance. That way you will be dissatisfied with yourselves and with your spouse. He will try to make sure married couples are too exhausted for physical intimacy and in that way they will be tempted to look elsewhere. He will emphasize mascots like Santa and the Easter Bunny for special holidays, that way the real meaning of the holidays is downplayed and minimized. He will keep us so busy working in our own power that we'll never know nor see God's power working in our life. He will make our lives seem so full with activity that we feel we have no time, nor space for God. And because everything is so fast-paced, it'll be easy to get caught in the minutia of life. It'll be easy to forget who we are, why we're here, and what's truly at stake. But if we know Satan's plans or at least his intentions, then we can better use that knowledge to be more strategic with how we go about things.

We should not underestimate the fact that Satan is "the god of this world", and as 2 Corinthians 4:4 tells us "The god of this age has blinded the minds of unbelievers…" But though Satan currently holds sway over the spiritual blindness of the lost, we who follow Christ have been rescued from his domain, delivered "from the dominion of darkness" and brought "into the kingdom of the God" as

Colossians 1:13 states. We must go about our days living in congruence with what the Bible teaches, resisting the devil, standing firm in the faith, and sharing the gospel that shatters spiritual blindness.

Because once the curtain has been pulled back, a full realization sets in. We are in this world but we are not of it. We should be treating it as a foreign land, filled with traps and decoys designed to ensnare and entangle us. We should be treading lightly, taking each step with calculated care and entrusting ourselves to the One who has already overcome the ruler of this world. That's how we honor God.

## Chapter 9 – The Flesh

*"The flesh is a relentless whisperer, tempting the soul with desires that fade as quickly as they burn, while the spirit longs for what endures beyond the fleeting pulse of passion."* -Author Unknown

Romans 8:6 says *"To be carnally-minded is death, but to be spiritual-minded is life and peace."* This word Carnal means the flesh, or this body we have while we're here on earth. And because we inhabit this body while we're here, it's easy to forget we are so much more. It's so easy to get trapped into thinking we are this body and so we want what the body wants.

We are so much more than what we see when we look at ourselves in the mirror. The body, this outward version of us is not who we really are. We are an immortal soul and a spirit that inhabit this body. The body is then, just like a vehicle, a tool we use. An instrument that allows us to get things done and to get from Point A to Point B. It can be used for good or for evil, for a positive outcome or a negative one. But tools, like anything else can be neglected or taken care of. They can be withered away by distraction and comfort or built up with discipline and guided for purpose. The choice in how we use this body is ultimately ours. But we must always remember, we are eternal spirits in a human body having a temporary experience.

This place is not, nor was it ever meant to be our home. We must treat it as foreign land, and we are just visiting for a short time. For some, their time here is shorter than others, but we must not get too comfortable. Because whether we are here for a year or another 80 years, we will inevitably leave this place. The question then becomes, where will we go after?

1 John 2:15-17 states "Love not the world, neither the things of the world. If any man love the world, the love of the Father is not in him. For all that is the world, the lust of the flesh, the lust of the eyes, and the pride of life, is not of the Father, but is of the world." In this verse there are specific instructions of what to die daily to. We must be crucifying the flesh daily and not giving into carnal desires. We must hold ourselves to a higher standard than the rest of the world does and keep ourselves accountable.

We must become mindful of what our eyes focus on because through them we bring about those desires into the heart. And we must strive to crucify our pride as this is the one thing that caused rebellion in Heaven amongst Satan and his followers. By exercising dominion over these things, we practice putting to death daily our sinful nature and in turn, begin to walk in victory over the flesh.

Fasting is one of the direct ways that we can "crucify the flesh." It's by intentionally denying bodily desires that allows us to focus on spiritual growth. It's about treating the body as a servant, and even though it may want something, and that desire keeps growing and growing, the body must obey whatever we, inside the body decide. The body is subject to what the mind decides, regardless of the feelings that arise. It's easy to forget this and fasting, whether it be from food, technology, or whatever you carnally want, is a way to remind yourself of who and what you truly are. In Galatians 5:24, Paul writes, "And those who belong to Christ Jesus have crucified the flesh with its passions and desires." Fasting is one way we do this. By saying no to the cravings of the body, we strengthen our spirit and align more closely with God's will. When you starve the body, you feed the spirit. Jesus Himself fasted for forty days in the wilderness (Matthew 4:1–2), setting a precedent for spiritual preparation, dependence on God, and victory over temptation. Furthermore, in Matthew 6:16–18, Jesus instructs His followers not if they fast, but when, implying that fasting is expected in the Christian walk.

Logically, fasting removes distractions, heightens spiritual sensitivity, and cultivates humility as it states in Psalm 35:13. It reminds us that man does not live by bread alone (Deuteronomy 8:3), and as we weaken the flesh, we make room for the Spirit to work more fully in our hearts, drawing us into deeper intimacy with God. And in Mark 9, it talks of a boy who was possessed, and the disciples were unable to remove the bad spirit from him. But Jesus easily removed it and told them that those types of demons can only be removed through fasting and prayer. So in order to achieve that level of dominion, fasting is required. If we believers can choose Christ over our greatest passions, the light that emanates from within us will be so bright that it will be able to help so many.

It's been said that whatever you feed will flourish. If you feed your faith, you will in turn starve your doubt. However, we've all seen far too many times where we feed both our faith and our doubts. We declare that we trust God but then speak about lack and limitation. That doublemindedness is what Satan strives for because it keeps us in that middle ground, where we are neither hot, nor cold. And that's a dangerous place for a believer to be. Because it leaves us open to so much demonic influence.

They say, "Stand for something because if you don't, then you'll fall for everything." We must be all in with no back-stepping. In Genesis 19, there is a story of Lot's wife. As God destroyed the wicked cities of Sodom and Gomorrah with fire and brimstone, Lot, his wife, and their daughters were allowed to escape. The only instruction from angels was not to look back. However, as they fled, Lot's wife disobeyed this command and turned to look back at the destruction. She was instantly transformed into a pillar of salt as a consequence of her disobedience and attachment to the sinful city. Her decision to look back cost her dearly.

God created everything, including all the angels. And he gave them free will as is demonstrated in their disobedience and rebellion against Him. This was a deliberate choice by some angels to oppose God and rebel. That's how great our God is that He allows choice, freedom, and will, so that there can be love and genuine relationship. True love cannot be forced; it must be chosen freely. In giving His creation, the freedom to obey or disobey, God showed that He values authentic relationship over control.

Even in the face of rebellion, His desire for connection and redemption remain steadfast. In the end, God's sovereignty is not diminished by our choices. It is revealed through His grace, patience, and unwavering love for those who turn back to Him. But it's on us to recognize the flesh is not our friend. It wants us living at the level of the material even though we now know there's so much more at play. It's what we do with what we now know that truly matters.

Let us be ever mindful that as Christians, we walk in the tension between flesh and Spirit. Though "we walk in the flesh" and our bodies are still subject to earthly weakness, we are called to wield spiritual weapons that break strongholds, not worldly strategies. We belong to Christ, and "those who belong to Christ Jesus have crucified the flesh with its passions and desires" as Galatians 5:24 tells us. It's a daily choice that we put on Christ, yield to the Holy Spirit, and allow His fruit to spring forth from us. Love, joy, peace, patience, kindness, goodness, faithfulness, gentleness, and self-control so that every thought, word, and action are guided according to Christ.

As we go about our days, we must remember that we step into the life Christ died to give us. And not by fleshly effort, but by Spirit-empowered surrender. May our journey be marked, not by the fading desires of the flesh, but by the eternal life and fruit of the Spirit.

## Chapter 10 - The Bible

*"A Bible that's falling apart usually belongs to someone who isn't."* – Charles Spurgeon

The Bible is one of the most influential books in human history. There's never been an archaeological discovery that has contradicted the truth laid out in the Bible. And there is not a truth in the Bible that if you apply to your life, your life does not dramatically improve. It is the "most accurate, transparent, historically robust account that one can have of the most important figure ever in the history of the world", Yeshua (Jesus Christ).

The bible provides a profound foundation for faith, offering guidance on morality, purpose, and humanity's relationship with God. It also inspires hope and transformation through its teachings on grace, forgiveness, and love.

Historically, the Bible is a record of ancient civilizations, chronicling pivotal events, cultural practices, and the development of religious thought. It has influenced art, literature, politics, and social movements across centuries. Prophetically, the Bible contains numerous fulfilled prophecies, lending credibility to its divine inspiration and offering a framework for understanding God's plan for the world. Its timeless relevance continues to inspire millions, transcending generations as a source of wisdom and hope.

Despite what Satan wants you to believe, the Bible isn't a book filled with fairy tales and fables. Demons are very real and we battle them everyday. The idea is to put on the full armor of God daily and stand up for ourselves and our family. The Armor of God, as described in Ephesians 6:10-18, is a powerful way we can defend, protect, and go on the offensive, to stand firm against Satan, his demons, and any evil that floods the spiritual realm. Because Satan is always on the lookout, seeking easy prey to devour, arming ourselves with this armor is important to overcome the schemes of the devil. And the Bible is foundational to it all.

This armor includes the Belt of Truth, which grounds us in God's reality. It represents honesty and integrity, holding everything together like a belt secures clothing. It's about living in alignment with truth, and truth is foundational in every regard. But because Satan always wants to invert the things of God, he will try to peddle lies as truth and truth as lies. That's why this piece of armor is vital in today's world.

It also includes the Breastplate of Righteousness which is designed to protect our hearts through a life aligned with God's will. It symbolizes a life of moral uprightness and faith, congruent with God's teaching. The idea is to protect the heart and vital organs from guilt and sin, much like a breastplate shields a soldier.

The Shoes of the Gospel of Peace enable us to walk confidently in faith. This also refers to a readiness to spread the message of Jesus and the Gospel, giving stability and mobility to stand firm against any and all attacks.

The Shield of Faith helps us deflect attacks of doubt, fear, and temptations, likened to how a soldier's shield helps him block attacks from his opponent.

The Helmet of Salvation secures our minds with the assurance of redemption. It's designed to protect our headspace, signifying the assurance of salvation and hope that keeps one grounded in their identity as saved.

The Sword of the Spirit is God's Word, which in essence, is The Bible, and acts as an offensive weapon to counter lies with truth and evil with good. It is the only offensive weapon in the armor and represents a familiarity with Scripture. This is why it is vitally important to read and study our Bibles daily.

 Satan and his demons know the Bible too, for they were once in Heaven in the presence of God. But because of their enmity towards God and His people, they will tweak scripture in such a way to make it false, but seemingly true. This is done to sway people away from God, and in turn, bring hurt to the Father. But someone who is familiar with their Bible can spot the inconsistencies and see the lies for what they are. Even when Jesus fasted for 40 days and Satan tried to tempt him, Satan used scripture that was tweaked to try and trick Jesus. But because Jesus knew the Bible, he was not to be tricked, but rather used scripture to overcome the devil. Every ploy that Satan used was an inversion of scripture, and Jesus saw right through it and served it right back in the correct, aligned, and accurate way.

So, in order to overcome Satan daily, and he will be on the prowl, attacking daily, we must put on this armor through prayer, scripture, and intentional living. Things must not be done on accident or in a haphazard way. We do this on purpose with the purpose of relying on God's strength rather than our own. By staying vigilant and equipped, we resist the enemy's attacks, finding victory in spiritual battles through faith and obedience. Paul emphasizes that prayer is the means to stay connected to God while "wearing" this armor and fighting this battle.

For centuries, the Bible was primarily accessible only to those who spoke and understood Hebrew, Aramaic, or Latin, as it was largely confined to those texts. This left most people reliant on clergy or scholars to read and interpret its teachings. This limited access restricted personal engagement with its wisdom and even revelation from the Holy Spirit. Today however, the Bible is the number one selling book of all time and is translated into thousands of different languages. Its messages of faith, morality, prophecy, and guidance are available to all. But it's useless if it's left unread on a shelf or in a box.

The Bible's power as a tool for personal growth and learning lies in its timeless lessons, that have stood the test of time. Even now, modern archaeological discoveries, such as ancient manuscripts and sites corroborating biblical accounts, continue to provide evidence supporting its historical reliability, reinforcing its enduring truth and relevance.

If my earthly father wrote a book filled with insights, instructions for living a good life, and a world view to follow, I'd read it as often and deliberately as possible. It would offer a unique window into the values, wisdom and experiences that could help me make this experience a more useful and enjoyable one. That's what the Bible is. It is inspired by our heavenly Father, God, and the information contained in it is designed to help us live at the level that God intended. And B.I.B.L.E. could easily stand for "Basic Instructions Before Leaving Earth." Afterall, that's pretty much what it's doing. We just have to take the time to read and study it. And then of course, do what it says.

# Part II – The Physical Side of This Battle

## Part II - Introduction

So, we've seen how Satan can enter our lives through the spiritual side and wreak havoc amongst many believers. But now let's look at how he is able to prime us for defeat in that battle by weakening our minds, debilitating our bodies, and softening our will. After all, if he can attack our minds, bodies, and will, he can better deploy his assault on us, keeping us in bondage to the things of this world, and separated from God. And because of his hatred and enmity towards God, he will go about this attack any and every which way. Because to him, this is very personal. And anything goes.

We must always be willing to truly consider evidence that contradicts our beliefs and admit the possibility that we may be wrong. Intelligence isn't so much about knowing everything but rather having the ability to challenge everything we know. It begins with recognizing that our knowledge and perspectives are often shaped by personal experiences that have been hammered in since an early age.

Cultural influences also play a role as some things are even too taboo to talk about, and even more so to question. And limited biased information that was designed to keep us disempowered but under the guise of contrary keeps us locked into the matrix. When we question what we hold to be true, we open the door to new insights and the possibility of uncovering hidden layers of truth. This encourages us to seek different types of viewpoints, and research thoroughly to test the validity of our ideas. Digging deeper requires an open mind and major discernment. Some of these truths laid out in this book may force you to re-evaluate what you already think of as true. But it is important to recognize that Satan has his hands in every aspect of human life in this place. Once you fully realize that, you begin to see this deliberate, systematic breakdown of our minds and bodies that has been happening for quite some time now.

The enemy knows that in order to deliver us from good and keep us away from God, he must attack the body, the brain and the spirit. He's been at this for generations, using the pretense of something noble to achieve that goal. This systematic attack is being done through our water, the food, the air, the medicine, and even the education system. If he can control what we eat, what we drink, what we breathe, and what we are taught, he can shape every aspect of our lives in the physical and keep us thinking that's all there is.

## Chapter 11 – The Media

*"In a world where truth is twisted and narratives are bought, the greatest weapon is not the lie itself, but the willingness of minds to believe it."* -Author Unknown

The most powerful tools in history use to be guns and bombs. But in this new age, information is the power and those who control the flow of it, can manipulate the minds who consume it. In 2013, then-President Obama helped pass something called the Smith-Mundt Modernization Act, which repealed the 1948 Smith-Mundt Act. The 1948 act prohibited releasing propaganda information in U.S. to the public. Basically it was illegal for the media or any company to push lies for truth, regardless if the end justified the means. With the passing of this "Modernization Act", propaganda became completely legal no matter how outrageous the propaganda would be.

Scripted and orchestrated false narratives would now be allowed to be given to the public as factual news by trusted news anchors and journalists. All the while, the public was oblivious to this and still believed everything that was said on TV. Afterall, it was said on the mainstream news channel and by one of their favorite "journalist".  By selectively reporting information, using emotionally charged language, or omitting key details, the media was now shaping public perception so that it could align with specific agendas. This included amplifying stories that distracted from critical issues, framing events to discredit dissenting voices, and prioritizing content that reinforced the narrative. But because an agenda was and is at play, it is important for believers to think for themselves, investigate critically, and use discernment to separate truth from falsehoods. And understand that almost everything we see on TV or hear from the media is a scripted performance with the purpose of shaping our world view to benefit the powerful interests running the show.

It's been said that it's easier to control a population that is under stress and fear than one that is not. The media, in collusion with major interest groups have a vested interest to keep the public divided, fearful, and unaware of what's truly happening around the world and in their backyards. In today's society, truth has increasingly become subjective, shaped by personal beliefs, biases, and the echo chambers of social media. Facts are often overshadowed by opinions, and people are more likely to embrace narratives that align with their worldview, regardless of their validity. This shift has blurred the line between objective reality and individual perception, creating divisions and challenges in achieving common understanding.

Lies today are often peddled as truth through the deliberate spread of misinformation and disinformation. This is being done on an ongoing basis through the manipulation of narratives and the gaslighting of truths. Falsehoods can easily gain credibility and reach vast audiences by biased reporting, exploited through all the major news media outlets. When repeated enough, these lies can take on the appearance of truth, influencing opinions and decisions while eroding trust in reliable sources. But just like Booker T. Washington once said, "A lie doesn't become truth, wrong doesn't become right, and evil doesn't become good just because it's accepted by the majority."

Lies are scared of truth. That is why they try to silence it, distract from it, or smear it. Because lies recognize that if the truth ever became realized by the masses, the domino effect would come into play and all the lies held up by one another would come crashing down. The whole house of cards would fall and a mass awakening would occur. So Satan, the father of lies, makes it his mission to keep the lies alive and well.

What does it mean when something that's been said has been taken off the internet? There's no difference between burning a book and taking something off the internet. Hours and hours of content on YouTube has been banned or scrubbed. Hundreds if not thousands or articles have been deleted or moved to an area where they cannot be found. The censoring of information on topics that act as foundational to other big picture topics has been astronomical. The domino effect that would ensue if full disclosure was to happen would topple so many other foundational "truths" with it. So, they scrub, delete, move, and hide results along with weaponizing terms to discourage people in their pursuit of truth. That's how book burning has transformed in this modern day and age.

It's all an attempt to erase history, silence dissent, or eliminate knowledge perceived as threatening. The equivalent of this is happening in real time today all over the internet. Information that is not aligned with the narrative is scrubbed or moved to the bottom of a search, making it nearly impossible to find. Anything that has been dubbed as a conspiracy theory or flagged by so called "Fact-Checkers" mysteriously disappears into the abyss of the internet. It's like that by design.

This idea of book burning has been a recurring symbol of censorship and suppression throughout history, often employed by those in power to control ideas and enforce ideological conformity.

The Mandela Effect is used as a psyop to make people feel and look crazy for believing something they know to be true, but all evidence has been erased from proving it. It's a phenomenon where a large group of people remember an event or detail differently from how it supposedly occurred or is recorded. They use it as a means to erase evidence and even introduce alternate reasons as to why memories may be skewed. They blame it on everything from parallel universes to alternate realities to flaws in psychology. And people jump on board with fascination and a hope that these are true. But if one were to scratch the surface on these, we'd see they're all designed to delete God from the equation and remove information from our timeline.

We are living in a time when the capability to research everything that is in question is at our fingertips. Albeit some information may be harder to find using the traditional search engines. So, adapting and using other types of search engines may be needed. But questioning everything that is mainstream should be a non-negotiable for all Christians. Especially since we know Satan has his hand in almost everything, as he is the god of this world. The goal is to understand what's really at play and how to go about it to make sound decisions. Hosea 4:6 says "My people perish for lack of knowledge; because thou hast rejected knowledge, I will also reject thee…" Lack of knowledge is why we perish, and we cannot be ignorant to the fact that it's on us to investigate.

Proverbs 4:7 says, "Wisdom is the principal thing; therefore get wisdom: and with all thy getting, get understanding." We must research, probe, inspect, and dig into whatever we are being told by mainstream media, authorities with an agenda, and so-called "experts." We are not to trust as Psalm 118:9 says "Put not your trust in the princes, in mortal men who cannot save. But we should "Trust in the Lord with all our heart and lean not unto our own understanding; in all our ways we should submit to Him, and he will make our paths straight" says Proverbs 3:5-6.

James 1:5 tells us "If any of you lacks wisdom, you should ask God, who gives generously to all without finding fault, and it will be given unto you." We must deliberately put ourselves back in the driver's seat because we cannot be a passive passenger, being taken wherever the vehicle goes. It's on us.

A lot of people like to describe our press as "free and open" because it is not owned by the state. But they ignore the fact that it is owned by six multinational conglomerates whose shareholders have a unified set of class interests that get reflected in almost all the media coverage. We must get back to what truth stands for and what it means to us as a society and to us personally. We can achieve this by going back to what our grandparents and great grandparents used to do daily. That is, reading of our Bibles. And not just reading it but studying it. Don't see it as a goal to go through it as fast as possible but rather see it as a way to unravel all the insight, principles, and truth it has to offer. The more you are able to connect with it and spend time in prayer, discernment begins to take shape. And discernment is the ability to distinguish between right and wrong, truth and deception, and is guided by wisdom and the Holy Spirit. Proverbs 3:21 encourages keeping sound wisdom and discretion, while Hebrews 5:14 speaks of mature believers who, through practice, have trained themselves to discern good from evil.

Discernment is essential for living a righteous life and aligning one's actions with God's will. Improving discernment involves cultivating wisdom, critical thinking, and spiritual awareness.

We do this by seeking God's guidance and praying for wisdom and clarity. James 1:5 says, "If any of you lacks wisdom, you should ask God, who gives generously. We can also study the scriptures because regularly reading and meditating on the Bible helps us to align thoughts and decisions with God's truth. In doing this, we begin to practice reflection because taking time to assess situations and decisions carefully is vital to our growth as believers.

We must always consider how our thoughts and decisions align with moral and spiritual principles. Because we know we are to be driven by a sound mind and not emotion. We start learning how to respond rather than react. And we begin to gain and accumulate knowledge by staying informed but with a mindfulness of where we get our information from. If we're constantly seeking to understand, we're better equipped to recognize truth and deception. And we strive to learn from experience by analyzing and reflecting on past decisions to better discern patterns and outcomes.

 Lastly, the bible tells us that we are to surround ourselves with wise counsel. Proverbs 1:5 tells us "Let the wise listen and add to their learning and let the discerning get guidance." Proverbs 12:5 states "The way of fools seems right to them, but the wise listen to advice." And Proverbs 15:22 says "Plans fail for lack of counsel, but with many advisers, they succeed."

So, when we engage with spiritually mature individuals who can offer insight and accountability, it allows us a different perspective and a better view on things. By integrating these practices, we can develop a sharper sense of discernment to navigate life and avoid pitfalls that were created through lies and disinformation. Pitfalls that were designed to keep us at the mercy of deception and to keep us as victims to societal woes.

In a world overflowing with information, and just as much misinformation, it's more important than ever for believers to walk in discernment. Because not everything labeled as "truth" is grounded in God's truth. That's why we must turn to the Bible as our ultimate standard, seek wise and godly counsel, and filter everything through prayer and the guidance of the Holy Spirit. God calls us to be vigilant, testing every spirit and holding fast to what is good as 1 Thessalonians 5:21 tells us. By staying rooted in His Word and surrounded by faithful believers, we can avoid the confusion of deception and stand firm in the truth that sets us free.

## Chapter 12 – The Internet of Things

*"The Internet of Things is not just about connecting devices— it's about unlocking intelligence in the everyday, turning data into decisions and objects into allies." – ChatGPT*

The Internet of Things (IoT) refers to a vast and growing network of physical devices, such as appliances, vehicles, sensors, and machines all connected to the internet. Because they are connected to the net, they're all capable of collecting and exchanging data. But to what end? Also called the Internet of Nano-Things, this technology has the potential to transform how we live and work.

And even though on the surface, this may seem like a good thing, it has implications that can have detrimental effects on all our lives. On paper, this will enable smarter homes, more efficient industries, and real-time insights that drive better decision-making. From wearable health monitors to automated farms, IoT can vastly improve convenience, safety, and productivity.

But the truth is, it's all about control. Privacy, security, and data can all be turned on us at a whim. And with AI now being able to manipulate pictures and video, a growing concern about what is real and what is not is only going to grow. In the court of public opinion, images can easily be manipulated to cause someone to look guilty when in fact they are not, or innocent when they're actually guilty. And that's just the start.

Many are calling The Internet of Things the Fourth Industrial Revolution. This rise of smart technologies are not merely about innovation and convenience. They are a foundation of a vast, global surveillance and control grid. Every connected device, from smart refrigerators to biometric wearables, to even vehicles, become a node in a network designed not only to collect data but to monitor and influence human behavior in real time. What appears to be about efficiency and progress is actually a carefully constructed system to track every movement, decision, and even thought.

This can easily lead to the forming of the infrastructure of digital control over mankind. In other words, this can pave the way for the framework that will eventually govern and dominate all of us.

Everything will be integrated into an ecosystem, driven by big data collecting, monitoring, and regulating. As of now, many of the systems are already in place. Smart phones along with wearable tech that have smart technologies such as smart watches and fitness trackers are already gathering data and using it for advertising and services. And they also pulse constant radiation affecting us at a cellular level that isn't always evident right away. But the accumulation of this radiation can have devastating effects in the long run.

New research shows that when we are wearing these technologies and our bodies get wet, either due to sweating, swimming, or weather, our bodies become better EMF conductors. EMF is short for electro-magnetic field which are physical fields that produce waves of radiation emitting from a source.

Smart Traffic lights are an example where IoT is at work. In theory, this can allow intersections to adapt and modify according to the flow of traffic. Camera systems located around intersections, are collecting data on traffic, vehicles, and vehicle owner information.

Smart medicine is in its early stages as the mRNA Covid Vaccine was a trial run, but the ultimate goal is to merge humans with technology, blurring the lines between the physical, digital, and biological realms. To create a type of medicine that becomes a part of our genome and in turn, become a part of us, always connected to the internet.

With that in place, they can actually more closely monitor us, study us, and even flip a switch to end us if they chose. Seems extreme and even not likely until we realize who really is the god of this world and how he continues to usurp his agenda of hurting God and bringing pain to His people.

Smart lightbulbs and smart appliances are also included in this because they are constantly monitoring, listening and recording everything done around them. Aside from privacy being violated, the question becomes, where and who is receiving this information. And for what reasons? And why would appliances and even lightbulbs need this sort of technology?

On a side note, LED bulbs are also having an affect on us due to micro-flickers, even if we don't consciously notice them. These flickers are rapid fluctuations in the light intensity that occur at a frequency too fast for the human eye to see, but they can still have an impact on our health and well-being. They are straining the eyes, affecting our sleep, impacting our mental health, and causing disorientation and fatigue. But because we aren't being told this by mainstream media, we just assume it's the stress of our job, or a sign of us getting older, or a problem in our genes. So, if you've been feeling a little off lately, look to the lights that are on around you.

New vehicles are now coming out with smart technologies as well, which in essence, gives them the capability to be monitored and controlled remotely. Think of car accidents that are not so accidental. Think of car malfunctions to restrict travel in the name of "climate change" and "global warming."

Social media and AI Language Models like ChatGPT and Grok are also tapping in and gathering data about their users. Psychology and behaviors are easily observed and recorded. Tendencies are revealed and patterns become apparent which opens the door to manipulation and control on a mass scale. And at the end of the day, most of the information provided through these avenues is still highly filtered to ensure it is aligned with the narrative deemed appropriate at the time. Information must be controlled even if it is through AI.

A recent article came out claiming the age of research papers and resumes is over due to the increase of use of AI technologies. The ability to write or create something using these tools is so easy, it's making it so that people don't rely on their own thinking and writing capabilities anymore. The immediate default is, let's ask ChatGPT. But aside from the information being highly filtered and selectively processed, it can create inherent problems with the way our minds and bodies are built. The premise is this: things we fail to use, we tend to lose. We stop using our legs, they atrophy and get smaller/weaker. We stop using our arms and the same thing happens. The very act of exercising something makes it stronger. So if we're not exercising our critical thinking skills, problem solving skills, and our analytical capabilities, they're slowly atrophying and getting weaker as time goes on.

Another study out of MIT shows brain scans of ChatGPT users after 4 months of use looking a lot different than non-users. ChatGPT users had brain engagement drop by 47%, memory retention was almost completely wiped out, and brains remained at a suboptimal level even after stopping AI use. The idea is this: if we are going to be using AI to replace our thinking, we're going to be weakening one of our greatest tools, which is our brain.

AI in and of itself is a tool that is inevitably here to stay. We must learn to adapt and use it strategically if we are to use it at all. But we cannot be lazy about its use, outsourcing all thinking capabilities to it. We must learn to think deeply for ourselves and then use AI as a strategic ally to enhance and not takeover. Because it's in the obstacles that we face that we grow and develop our capacity to adapt and overcome. That's how God created us, it's by design.

Deceptive images and deep fake videos are starting to emerge, making it harder to tell what's real and what's fake. A new study came out and showed "baby boomers" were the most likely to believe fake AI videos. But with technology is this area growing at exponential speeds, it's only a matter of time where it's all hyper-realistic and no one will be able to tell the difference.

At the moment, there are tell-tale signs that give away the video as fake. Glitches in the frame, things morphing from one thing to another, audience members having 2 faces or 6 fingers, and automobiles with 2 front sides, one on the front and another in the back. These are all examples of some of those signs that can be spotted if thoroughly looked for. But even a computer-generated voice over acting as a reporter talking about things that were allegedly said and done can be quickly fact-checked to find that none of what was mentioned in the video was factual. Despite these signs of sham, social media apps such as TikTok and Meta are now becoming inundated with these fake AI videos designed to create misinformation, division and discord.

The last of these smart technologies will be in the form of smart cities, also known as 15-minute cities. These are aimed at making cities more livable, sustainable, and community-focused by ensuring that everything a person needs is within a 15-minute radius. Work, shopping, education, healthcare, food, and recreation are all to be accessible by walking or a bike ride from their home.

On paper, the goal is to reduce dependence on cars, cut emissions, strengthen local economies, and enhance quality of life. They tell us it's about walkability, sustainability, and a greener future. But what happens when convenience becomes forced confinement? With surveillance cameras on every corner, the possibility of digital id checkpoints, and every move being tracked, control becomes more attainable. Miss a curfew, travel too far or dissent too loudly and you may find yourself locked out of services, or worse.

The implementation of traffic filters can limit movement within zones. Smart grid tech can be turned on or off remotely depending on your conformity. Facial recognition and AI policing can keep track and monitor your every move. Suddenly this urban Utopia starts looking more like a prison. What if the real plan isn't so much about saving the planet but to cage the people and maintain complete control.

The Great Reset is an idea put forth by the World Economic Forum to restore the planet's carbon footprint by digitizing everything. They have been quoted as saying "Everything that can be digitized will be digitized." According to the experts, when everything is digitized, it will create less waste and more efficiency. It's all about bringing together the digital, physical, and biological systems and having them work synchronously.

Through AI, brain-computer interfaces, digital ID systems, and centralized control of digital currencies, society is being nudged toward a total dependency on technology. This dependency may set the stage for the One World Government that the Bible warns us of. It can easily take the form of this global technocracy where dissent is quickly silenced, privacy is virtually eliminated, and freedom is redefined as compliance.

From a biblical prophecy standpoint, this trend is seen as the slow but steady march toward the "Mark of the Beast" described in Revelation 13. As global systems of commerce, identification, and movement become digitized and unified, a time may come when participation in society requires allegiance to a singular authority. This mark, interpreted by some as a form of biometric ID, implantable chip, or digital credential like a barcode, will, according to the prophecy, be required to "buy or sell." Those who refuse may be cut off from the system, persecuted, or worse.

For many watching these developments through a prophetic lens, the convergence of IoT, smart technologies, and centralized digital governance appears to be not just a coincidence, but the fulfillment of ancient warnings. And yet, we march forward not fully grasping the implications that lie ahead.

## Chapter 13 – Water

*"Water is the driving force of all nature. It is not only essential for life but also a silent guardian of survival, nourishing every living being and sustaining the balance of our world."* — Adapted from Leonardo da Vinci

Water is another area we are constantly being attacked on. Satan has this enmity towards God and his people that he wants to take away their health, their higher thinking attributes, and everything else that makes them aware of truth. Our ability to think critically and to connect with God spiritually are the main targets for this assault.

So how does he do this? Since water is something so essential for our bodies to survive and it makes up a large portion of our earthly bodies, it makes sense that Satan can use this need to sneak in some things that can derail the natural balance our bodies require. The premise is simple, if the intake of water is bad, the cumulative effect on the body will then be bad. At that point, frailty, feebleness, and docility will be the result.

But many of us just assume that water is water, and that we should be drinking more of it. But where we get our water matters more than how much we are really drinking. Most of us take for granted where the water that runs through our homes comes from. We are just happy that we have water when we turn the faucet on or flush the toilets. But if we were to look into how that water gets there, how it's processed, and how it's essentially recycled, we'd have a better perspective on that water, what it really contains and how it affects our bodies.

Water Treatment Plants that distribute water for each city have a basic way of filtering out major contaminants but are neither efficient nor very effective in doing so. For the stuff they can't filter out, they add chemicals as a means to disinfect that water. One of the many issues with that is that those chemicals, such as Chlorine, Chloramine, and Trihalomethanes, tend to react with organic matter and can easily accumulate in our bodies. This leads to unnecessary stress on organs used to detoxify the body, tissues where the accumulation occurs, and the nervous system that processes information. And because these things don't only get absorbed through eating and drinking but also through the skin, this consistent exposure to water and the chemicals in it cause a build up that can manifest as a bunch of different ailments later on in life.

Fluoride is something else often added to public water supplies and is done under the guise that it's healthy and prevents tooth decay. This practice has been endorsed by numerous health organizations as a safe and effective way to improve dental health. However, there are ongoing debates about the potential health risks of long-term fluoride exposure. Just recently, Fluoride was categorized as a Neurotoxin even though many already knew of the harmful effects and were trying to warn the rest of us.

Studies are now revealing that it does lower IQ, delays brain development, and affects cognitive capacity. In essence, it's dumbing us down, diminishing our intellectual output and lowering our critical thinking capacity. It's also calcifying the Pineal Gland which is vital in many body processes. The pineal gland produces Melatonin, regulates sleep-wake cycles, regulates biological rhythms, is involved with intuition, and many believe it plays a major role in the body-spirit connection.

Other compounds that are commonly found in water nowadays are Arsenic, Chromium, Lead, Aluminum, Hormones, Nitrates, Pesticides, and even pharmaceutical drugs. All of these things are persistent and difficult to filter out through conventional means. This means that even though water treatment facilities try to clean out the water the best they can, these compounds stay intact in the water, continuing to flow through the system.

And since most of the water that flows through system is recycled and reused, these compounds linger and accumulate in the water supply. This means that the water we use to wash dishes, to wash our clothes, to flush the toilet and to bathe, all goes down the drain and back to the treatment plant to be cleaned and reused. You can imagine when prescription drugs and other chemicals are flushed down the toilet and where they end up. Because those medicines and drugs cannot be filtered completely out.

Even people who are on chemotherapy, immunotherapy, or hormone therapy. The byproducts of what they are taking are still in active form when they leave their bodies. So, when they relieve themselves in the toilet, those products go back into that water treatment plant and are recycled back into our homes.

So the recycling of these compounds continues and the biomagnification gets exaggerated to the point where we are unknowingly taking in all kinds of pharmaceuticals. And no one really knows the long-term effects of this, especially in babies, toddlers, teens, and older adults. What we do know is that all of these chemicals are involved in hormone disruption, fertility reduction, DNA modification, neurological degradation and Gut Biome destruction.

The good news is our bodies are wonderfully made and do a marvelous job of metabolizing and eliminating things that are not good for it. In Genesis 1:26 it states that God said "Let us make man in our image." This phrase suggests that humans are created with certain qualities that reflect God's nature and His glory. When God created man, he designed them with unique systems in place that work based off "feed-in/feedback loops."

For example, when we are exposed to the sun, our skin produces Vitamin D. When we eat, the body breaks down those foods and distributes the nutrients accordingly where they need to be stored or used. The Pancreas releases insulin to help drive nutrients into their prospective places. Water is used as a solvent to drive out toxins from the body and hydrate our cells. Our liver detoxifies the body and produces Cholesterol to support cell membranes, hormone levels, and brain function. Whenever we get a cut, the body goes into action to heal it on its own. No effort on our part is needed. When there is an infection, a fever kicks in to fend it off and rid the body of the pathogens causing it. When we are overly hot, the body sweats to cool itself off. When we are cold, the body shivers to warm itself up. All of these are based on those systems that God endowed us with that glorify His foresight, knowledge, and divination. There is no effort on our part needed. Our bodies adapt and adjust to a variety of things and it's all by God's design in that "feed-in/feedback loop.

Problems arise however, when the things that are being introduced to the body are not naturally occurring or found in nature. Whenever something that is man-made, synthetic, or chemically concocted, the body struggles to break it down or use it for good. When this happens, these things tend to accumulate in our tissues and organs. And eventually systems can become over-burdened and overwhelmed. At that point dis-ease tends to show up and many times manifests as a bunch of other things.

The problem is that disease gets labeled something different and is attributed to something different. So connecting the dots to synthetic chemicals being taken in by food and water rarely gets investigated. But when one digs deep, they'll find either a lacking of essential nutrients or an accumulation of harmful substances that's ultimately causing the disease. When you get to that conclusion, things become easier to deal with. The solution becomes more clear.

They are attacking the body through a bunch of different ways but the intention is the same. Satan intends to destroy the mind and body of God's people before they can realize God's calling for their life. A calling that encompasses worship, obedience, witness, service, and discipleship. In order to accomplish this, we must have a mind and a body that is able and willing. We were never supposed to be filled with sickness and disease. The body God equipped us with has many systems in place to maintain health and adapt to whatever challenges it faces. But because Satan's infiltration into so many aspects of human life, we are conditioned to believe that many of the illnesses that beset us are normal and just a part of aging naturally. But what if it was in part because of what we are putting into our bodies? Afterall, because water is vital to the proper functioning of our bodies, it makes sense that we should be drinking more of it. We just need to be more mindful of where that water is truly coming from. Because what's in our water matters more than how much water we take in.

## Chapter 14 – Pesticides

*"We are living in a world where the chemical environment is being changed by man without full knowledge of the consequences, and the pesticide problem is only one facet of a much larger issue."* — Rachel Carson

Pesticides are substances designed to control, repel, or eliminate pests that threaten crops, livestock, and human health. On paper, they play a critical role in modern agriculture. We use them to ensure a stable food supply, increase agricultural efficiency, and minimize economic losses for farmers. Beyond farming, pesticides also help manage disease-carrying pests, like mosquitoes when cities go on spraying sprees. While the use of pesticides seems to have clear benefits, the consequential effects are becoming overwhelmingly evident.

The companies that make them do have alternatives that offer sustainability and safety. But there's far more profit in the status quo, and so these companies continue using materials that are affecting us and our children more than we realize.

Atrazine is the second most used herbicide right after Glyphosate and both are being found in our water supplies in quantities that far exceed recommended safety levels. If in a lab, Atrazine is added to a tank full of frogs, it will feminize every frog in that tank. And at least 10% of the male frogs will turn into fully viable female frogs, able to produce viable eggs. If it's doing that to frogs, there's a lot of other evidence that it can be doing that to humans as well. It's no wonder that in our society, Gender

Dysphoria is on the rise and the amount of teens and adults seeking to transition are at levels never before seen.

Satan takes great pride in glorifying this "disconnect" as this is a big insult to God. Genesis 1:27 says, "God created mankind in his own image, in the image of God he created them, male and female he created them." He calls us as male and female and that means that we are embodied creatures. That has an implication that God knows what he was doing when he created you and knew you before you were formed.

Satan is the one who came in and brought about confusion and corruption. He did it through these chemicals and then through social conditioning. The idea was to rationalize falsehoods and invert truth so that what is wrong seems right and what is bad seems normal. We are living in a sinful Genesis 3 kind of a world and like Proverbs 14:12 states, "There is a way that seemeth right unto man, but the end thereof are the ways of death." Our bodies matter eternally to God and so it matters what we do with our bodies now.

Glyphosate is that other herbicide and is the main ingredient in Round Up, a popular weedkiller. This stuff is sprayed all over the place to stop invasive weeds from hindering crop production and is extensively applied to genetically modified crops designed to resist its effects. The issue that arises is that this stuff doesn't biodegrade like other things. Glyphosate residues often remain in harvested crops long after they're picked and sold, contaminating the food supply. Washing this residue off is also no easy task, but an essential one. Runoff from treated fields introduces this toxin into waterways, polluting drinking water sources and other crops that are exposed to this water. Studies have linked glyphosate exposure to adverse health effects, including Cancer, developmental effects, gastrointestinal effects and skin issues. Its impact on soil health and biodiversity further exacerbates ecological imbalances, but yet variations of it are still in use today.

Pesticides in general pose significant risks to human health. They have been linked to all sorts of ailments from cancer to neurological disorders and even hormonal disruptions. Our bodies are being attacked and many of us are sitting back and acting as if it's not. We have to see it for what it is and start acting on it with a generational vision. Because this stuff is affecting us, our children, and eventually our children's children. It's on us to ensure a safer future for the generations to come.

## Chapter 15 – Food

*"Let food be thy medicine and medicine be thy food."* —
Hippocrates

GMO, which stands for Genetically Modified Organism, is a term that is becoming more and more common in today's world. The exact definition of a genetically modified organism and what constitutes genetic engineering varies but in essence, it means the genome of a specific food has been tampered with for the purpose of producing a higher yield with less effort and resources. They tend to make these foods more resistant to certain things, like pests, drought, or any other thing that might affect its viability. Sometimes they alter the genome of a food to make it more appealing to the eye, or to the palate. However, when food is modified in such a way, it becomes more difficult for the body to process and metabolize it. This usually translates into some kind of deficiency, disorder, disease, or even a Cancer.

Obviously, this does not happen overnight. As it's been stated, the human body is such a remarkable machine that God created with systems in place to adapt and modify for almost every type of situation it is confronted with. However, over time, the accumulation of toxins, modified foods, and chemicals can begin to show up in the body as some form of disease.

Apeel is a company that creates "plant-based" coatings designed to extend the shelf life of fresh fruits and vegetables. Their technology supposedly adds an extra layer of protection to the produce's surface, helping reduce food waste and maintain freshness. Despite FDA approval, some concerns have been raised. They have not fully disclosed all the formulation details so even though it states that it is plant-based, who knows what else is on the ingredients list. The coating is designed to be water resistant, so it is that much harder to wash off or clean the produce. This reduces our control over what we actually ingest. And at the end of the day, this is a form of a modified coating on a natural food. And once this happens, that natural/organic food is not longer natural/organic.

There are no long-term studies showing Apeel's safety in human consumption. What is known is that when the body is exposed to things that do not necessarily come from nature, the body struggles in metabolizing them. This leads to all types of issues that later become illnesses and then disease. And since this technology is fairly new, no one really knows how our bodies will respond to this coating or how the diseases will manifest.

Senomyx was founded in 1999 by Lubert Stryer, a prominent biochemist. The company develops patented flavor enhancers by using "proprietary taste receptor-based assay systems." These receptors have been previously expressed in HEK293 cells, which are human embryonic kidney cells. These cells originally came from a healthy, electively aborted human fetus in the early 1970s. The number 293 in the HEK means that 292 babies were killed before they finally got the cell line they wanted to use. In a lab setting, they replicate these cell lines and put them in these products as a means to enhance flavor. By studying the human genome sequence of these cell lines, Senomyx has identified hundreds of taste receptors and currently own 113 patents on their discoveries. With that, Senomyx collaborates with seven of the world's largest food companies to further their research and to fund development of their technology. This is why we find their technology in all types of foods from soft drinks to coffees to creamers to hydration drinks to chips to cereal to soup.

Artificial Dyes such as Red 40, Blue 1, Yellow #5 and Yellow #6 are food colors added to food and candy of all kinds to enhance the look and appearance of those foods. Yellow Dye #5 comes from something called Tartrazine and was originally made out of a sludge that's left over when you turn coal into coke for blast furnaces. We know it as coal tar and it was being found all over the place. Because it was very toxic and harmful to both the environment and to human health, everyone was trying to figure out ways to dispose of it.

A century ago, it was just an obnoxious industrial byproduct that everybody was trying to figure out ways to get rid of or put it to use. They began using it to build and pave roads. Then a British scientist figured out that this tar could be used to make fabric dye. As you can imagine, the next logical step would be to begin coloring the foods we eat, because it worked so well with fabrics. Food manufacturers began using it to mask the discoloration of low quality foods.

They may not have known back then that just this dye alone causes Asthma, tumors, developmental delays, neurological damage, ADD/ADHD, hormone disruption, gene damage, Anxiety, Depression, and intestinal injuries. And that's just from this one dye. The others too cause all sorts of issues in human health, and more so in children who are still developing.

Some countries have banned these additives from being in their foods and so these companies have adapted by not using them where they're not allowed. The question then becomes, why use them at all? Today, yellow dye is now made from petroleum, not coal tar, but the damage is still there. Either way, the addition of food dyes to our foods, candies, drinks, vitamins, and even our medicines should not be in place.

By design, they don't change or add to the flavor, but rather only change the color and appearance, making foods look more appealing. But they do come with hidden health risks as studies are now linking them to hyperactivity in children, allergic reactions, and potential long-term effects such as cancer and hormonal disruptions. Despite their widespread use in processed foods, the risks outweigh the benefits. Choosing natural alternatives and avoiding artificially colored foods can help protect our health and well-being.

Nutrient deficiencies today are at an all-time high. And these deficiencies cannot be fixed with a drug or medication. Drugs can be used to manage the symptoms associated with these deficiencies, which is better than suffering from the disease itself, but it will not address the real issue. The real issue is, the more whole grains you eat, the harder it is for your body to absorb the nutrients that your stomach just digested. "So not only are the foods minerally deficient because the soil is minerally deficient, but your body's ability to absorb what little nutrition there is in the food is extremely compromised." This is because we are listening to the same people who make the food giving us advice on what foods we actually need to be eating. That's a deadly combination and it's happening all over food industry and the pharmaceutical industry. This, among a few other things, is why chronic disease seems to be accelerating at the rate it is today. And why cures are far and few between, but medications to manage the illness are far and wide.

Highly processed foods loaded with chemicals, additives, and synthetic ingredients are masquerading as real food all throughout our society. Foods with Aspartame, BHA, BHT, High Fructose Corn Syrup, MSG, Propylparaben, Sodium Nitrate, TBHQ and Titanium Dioxide are all FDA approved and generally regarded as safe. But are they really? We have forgotten that food is information that controls gene expression, hormones, and metabolism. When the right foods are eaten, blood sugar is balanced, hormonal balance is restored, and stress' damaging impact is reduced.

Contrary to popular belief, regulatory agencies do not always have the general public's interests when it comes to safety in food science. When one takes a closer look at industry influence and lobbying efforts, a troubling pattern emerges. Most of the same agencies tasked with protecting public health are heavily influenced, if not directly compromised by big businesses. One of the more concerning mechanisms behind this is the GRAS loophole. GRAS stands for Generally Regarded As Safe and allows companies to self-certify new substances as safe without independent testing or oversight. As a result, thousands of synthetic compounds have entered our food, air, water and household products with minimal long-term safety testing. And it's all done in the name of making food more efficient, better looking, longer lasting, and better tasting. But the cost is becoming burdensome.

Food has the power to change every cell in the body for good and for bad. This stuff that was meant to nourish and sustain us, has become a hidden source of harm due to the widespread use of chemicals, additives, and processing methods.

From pesticides and artificial dyes to preservatives and endocrine-disrupting compounds, there are so many harmful substances making their way into our daily diets without our awareness. It's time we become more aware and defensive. Attacks are coming from all angles but we can minimize our exposure, and one way is by being mindful of what we eat. That's how we start gaining ground in this physical battle we're all facing.

## Chapter 16 - Endocrine Disruptors

*"The dose does not always make the poison when it comes to endocrine disruptors—low doses can sometimes be more harmful than high ones."* -Dr Frederick vom Saal

The Endocrine system is a system that modulates and regulates hormones responsible for growth, metabolism, reproduction, and other vital functions. Because hormones affect so many functions of the body, any time they are altered, the effects can have a dramatic and lasting effect. So, as you can imagine, the Endocrine System is vital to the proper functioning of the human body. Anything that can disrupt this vitally important system can cause a cascade of issues that may not seem connected to this system at all.

Endocrine Disruptors are synthetic or natural chemicals that interfere with the body's Endocrine System. They are commonly found in everyday items like plastic containers, food packaging, personal care products, household cleaners, pesticides, and even in the water supply. Examples include Bisphenol A (BPA), phthalates, dioxins, and microplastics.

The biggest culprits are absorbed through the skin daily such as arm deodorant and colognes/perfumes. Second to those are what we're putting into our bodies. Compounding this issue is the fact that Endocrine Disruptors are pervasive and persistent. They accumulate in the environment and in human tissue, creating chronic exposure risks that do not biodegrade or are detoxed very easily.

When taken in, these chemicals tend to mimic and alter natural hormones such as Estrogen, which is a female hormone and Testosterone which is a male hormone. In essence, they can make females start looking and acting like men. And they can make men start looking and acting like women. This rise in more and more men having female tendencies and women having male tendencies is climbing and is becoming more evident in our youth today.

The masculinization of women and de-masculinization of men is impacting the youth more than any other group in history. And many believe it may not be by accident. This disruption in the hormone levels of individuals is causing a massive wave of puberty disruptions, fertility challenges, homosexuality and psychological disorders.

Never has there been a time where more people have felt like they were born in the wrong body and needed a sex change operation to fix it. As if saying God made a mistake when he created them even though Jeremiah 1:5 states "Before I formed you in the womb I knew you, before you were born, I set you apart."

At one point, it was even declared "hate speech" if you wouldn't call someone by their preferred pronouns. This gender pseudo-science spread quickly like a mind virus that was designed to drown out sanity and logic. This idea of "pride" that was pushed by LGBTQ activists was even celebrated by legacy media and certain political parties. Ironically enough, the Bible speaks of pride as being the reason Satan and a third of the angels were cast out of Heaven.

The rainbow, which is the symbol at pride festivals and the LGBTQ rallies was a coincidently a symbol used to signify God's covenant with humanity. It was used as a reminder of God's mercy, His promise to preserve life, and His faithfulness to His word. It symbolized both the end of the flood and the assurance that God's judgment in that form would not come again. It serves as a reminder of God's mercy, faithfulness, and the promise of peace between God and humanity, as well as all living creatures. The appearance of the rainbow in the sky is a divine sign of hope and assurance for Noah and for all generations that follow.

It's funny though how Satan always wants to invert all that God made to be good, and he uses people that unknowingly are serving him at the physical level to accomplish that end. These inversions cause people to be led astray, misguided and deceived. And they fight tooth and nail for their deception.

Back to the message at hand. Exposure to these Endocrine disrupting chemicals has been linked to hormone-sensitive cancers such as breast, ovarian, and prostate cancers. Reproductive issues like infertility and decreased sperm quality are also dramatic effects being seen. Children with developing body systems are especially vulnerable, as exposure may lead to permanent developmental delays, immune dysfunction and cognitive impairments.

Long-term effects at any age also include an increased risk of metabolic disorders such as obesity, Diabetes, and thyroid dysfunction, as well as cardiovascular diseases. And for the elderly, whose hormone regulation is already declining, Endocrine Disruptors can exacerbate age-related issues like bone loss or cognitive decline, which is amplifying existing health risks.

Skin is major area where Endocrine Disruption is occurring on a massive scale. The reason for this is because skin is the largest organ of the human body and is excellent at absorbing substances directly into the blood stream. But because we were never taught anything about this, we nonchalantly put stuff all over our skin with no second thought. We use sunscreen to prevent sun damage. We use anti-aging creams to prevent premature aging. We use antiperspirant deodorant to prevent sweat and odor from seeping through our shirts. We use cologne and perfume to help us smell better. Women use make-up to beautify their faces. Men use hair gel to comb their hair.

All of these things may be done with the best of intentions, and we want to trust in the companies that make these products. But we need to look into how they can affect us at a micro and a macro level and begin reading ingredient labels. DNA damage, disruption of hormones, lower fertility, and internal flora destruction are all consequences as a result of these things that we put on our skin. And just because the effects are not so obvious at first, the damage being done accumulates, and before long, all types of issues begin to manifest in our bodies. But to the undiscerning, it's just a natural part of life, and is to be embraced as part of aging. But is it really?

What we know as Science is and has been for sale for quite some time. Researchers are given grants by governments and drug companies to come up with results that are aligned with the end result they initially wanted to have. If the results they come up with do not match their expected outcome, the funding through the grants is quickly pulled, and money stops flowing almost immediately.

Without the funding, the work eventually stops, forcing researchers to find other means to make a living. In essence, grants are what drive the Science, and in today's world, the Science cannot survive without the funds. So, if one wants to be a scientist, they need to ensure they set up the study in such a way that the results are congruent with what the funding companies want them to be. That's how products continue to be on the shelves and how narratives are maintained.

Objectivity often takes a back seat to profitability, and inconvenient findings are either buried or reframed. In this system, scientific integrity can be compromised, not necessarily by ill intent, but by the subtle pressures of staying funded and staying relevant. As a result, the public is left trusting "the Science" without realizing how deeply that "Science" was influenced by those holding the purse strings.

There are 27 companies that control the Military Industrial Complex, 30 companies control the entire medical industry, 10 companies control the food supply, and 6 companies control the flow of information. When so much is controlled by so few, it's easy to see how profit can be a motivating factor behind decisions. 1 Timothy 6:10 tells us "The love of money is the root of all evil." That love of money can be a powerful and blinding force, often driving values to be compromised. In the relentless pursuit of profit, ethical lines get blurred, shortcuts get taken, and safety studies get skewed. And it's us who pay the price.

This is why reading labels and understanding ingredients is a crucial step in protecting our health, especially in a world where endocrine disruptors are found in countless everyday products.

By taking the time to read labels and recognize potentially harmful ingredients, we can empower ourselves to make safer choices. Awareness is the first line of defense. And when we know what's in the products we use, we can avoid substances that may negatively impact our hormones and overall well-being. And in doing that, we can maintain this temple that is our bodies in the best shape possible to do the work that God has called us to do.

## Chapter 17 – Chemical Skies

*"Man-made climate change is what we really need to worry about – The stuff that is being done in the skies above us all."* - Author Unknown

The deliberate spraying of the skies with chemicals to supposedly modify the weather or block out the sun has been in place for a long time. It's gone by different names such as Cloud Seeding, Geoengineering, Climate Engineering, Solar Radiation Management, Stratospheric Aerosol Injection and as of late, commonly referred to as Chem Trails. Their outward goal is to combat climate change and that's how they've been able to get away with doing it for so long.

We are officially told by government agencies and the entire scientific community that climate engineering operations are only a proposal. We are told that if Climate Engineering, Geoengineering, or Solar Radiation Management Programs were to be deployed, it would be a last-ditch measure against the unfolding climate collapse. But according to them, nothing is in play as of now, even though there are over 1,100 patents for some variation of weather manipulation.

One of the bigger lies ever perpetrated on populations all over the world is the condensation trail lie, otherwise known as Con Trails. What we're seeing in the skies today is not condensation but rather sprayed particulate dispersion with few exceptions. Con Trails do not linger, dissipate, and develop into cloud coverage. Con Trails occur naturally because of cold air in high altitudes react with Carbon Dioxide and water vapor in the exhaust, creating ice crystals. Those ice crystals are what planes usually leave in their wake as they're flying across the sky. However, these types of ice crystals easily dissolve, and the trail left behind quickly dissipates. Many of the trails that are lining our skies today, which are usually seen in a crisscross pattern or even checkerboard pattern, are not normal nor natural. They are Chemtrails.

This term "Chemtrails" happens to be mentioned by name in House Bill 2977 back in 2001 under the Space Preservation Act even though the military denies any such program exists. As you can imagine, this doesn't get much publicity or press attention but the fact that it's on the record should speak volumes.

The definition of weather modification is "any activity performed with the intention of producing artificial changes in the composition, behavior, or dynamics of the atmosphere. So anytime stuff is injected into the atmosphere for the purpose of modifying weather, it is weather modification, even if all the internet search engines say otherwise. And once weather is injected with particulates for the purpose of changing it, it becomes one big science experiment and we are all the Guinea Pigs experiencing it.

Global dimming, also called Solar Dimming, is another term that refers to the amount of direct sunlight that no longer is able to reach the surface of where we live. Light scattering particles are being placed and building up in the atmosphere and they limit how much sun actually makes it to the surface. They tell us those particles are the byproducts of gas and jet engines that accumulate in the air but the truth is, those particles are deliberately being sprayed up there. They're not there by accident.

The newest method of this weather modification experiment is through something called S.A.T.A.N., which stands for Stratospheric Aerosol Transport And Nucleation. It's just a fancy yet sinister way of saying they are injecting particulates into the air for the purpose of modifying the weather. Even though FAA Regulation 9115 states that "No pilot in command of a civil aircraft may allow any object to be dropped from that aircraft in flight that creates a hazard to persons or property," it's still happening across the U.S. today.

Some high-altitude planes are now being equipped with technology designed to turn the sprayers on and off at the push of a button. This can allow the pilots to be more selective about where the spray is released and can also make it seem like the trails being created are more natural.

It turns out, they are spraying 10's of millions of tons of reflective toxic heavy metal and polymer particulates into the atmosphere annually. This creates artificial clouds that line the sky, disperse very slowly, and become hazy cloud formations that usually result in abnormal weather patterns in the days following.

The streaks across the sky, the irregular cloud formations, and the muddled haze that fills the atmosphere are evidence to what is happening all around us. To even mention this a few years ago would have you labeled a conspiracy theorist with no real evidence, nor backing. This is despite the numerous patents and demonstrations shown in the news, tv shows, and even legit scientific articles that show it's really happening. Plus, the evidence of our own eyes tells us these clouds today are not the same ones we'd see when we were kids. And the weather patterns are unlike what we'd see back then as well.

Depending on how you search for this phenomenon, you can get a wide variety of responses. If you type in Chem Trails into the search bar, you get articles immediately labeling it as "conspiracy theory" and "not proven." But if you type in Cloud Seeding, you get articles, published papers, and videos confirming it's use. Even though they are euphemisms of one another, and they mean the same thing, how you go about your quest for real information makes a difference. And because information flows from 5 major corporations, it's imperative that we begin to investigate and discern at a higher level. We cannot just accept what we are told because not everything is as it seems.

All sorts of nano particulates such as sulfates, heavy metals, Aluminum, Barium, Cadmium, Lead, Lithium, Mercury, along with various types of Bacteria, Viruses, Mold and even Fungus are in these mixtures being sprayed in the skies.

 In 1977, there was a senate hearing that confirmed 239 populated areas had been deliberately contaminated by biological agents between 1949 and 1969. San Francisco Bay was one of those areas in 1950. 2 species of bacteria, Bacillus globii and Serratia marcescens, were tested in that area via aerosol spraying.

The objective was never made clear but the fact that the public was never made aware of that experiment until these Senate Hearings came out showed they had some nefarious objectives. The question then becomes, why would Mold, Fungi, Viruses, and Bacteria be needed to combat Climate Change? Was there another agenda at play?

Even though they now admit it and use this idea of combatting climate change as the excuse, there cannot be a scientific reason behind so many of these chemicals and biologics. The rate that these things dissipate are dependent on weather, climate, wind, and atmospheric pressure. But because these things are very fluid and are always changing, it proves it's all just one big experiment. And we are the test subjects.

The sulfates, metals, and organic matter being sprayed into the sky also tend to end up in the crops, soil, wastewater treatment plants, reservoirs, and on the livestock. So even if a food is labeled "Organic", can it really be organic with so many chemicals falling on it from above. Anything that is on the surface of a food can easily be absorbed by that food and saturation can easily occur.

Shouldn't it be considered that every breath we take is littered with highly toxic particles that are wreaking havoc in our bodies. For example, Barium, one of the many particulates being found in the formations, can lead to stomach pains, chest pains, blood pressure problems, to even wearing down the immune system. So, issues that begin to manifest in the body due to these things can easily be attributed to something else, and the dots keep going un-connected. And this is just one of the many toxic chemicals, particles, and biologics being found in the spray that lines our skies.

These particles are not being reported by any air quality control testing systems. And the reason behind that is because those testing systems are looking for particles the size of 2.5 microns or bigger. But the nano-particulates being used in this spraying are exponentially smaller and go virtually unreported. These nano-particles create reactive oxygen species in biologic materials, which damages tissue, lead to advanced aging, cause skin conditions, create pulmonary illnesses, lead to neurodegenerative diseases like dementia, affect cognitive functioning, and can even cause cancer.

So aside from these toxins getting into the foods we eat, we're also getting bathed at a microscopic level. These particulates are landing on us not only through the morning dew, ground level fog, the condensation throughout the mornings and evenings, the mist and even the rain. We are being inundated with these particles that have no real long-term study on their safety, or reasoning for their purpose, but no one seems to mind or notice.

1 Thessalonians 5:6 says "So let us not sleep, as others do, but let us keep awake and be sober." Proverbs 4:23 states "Keep your heart with all vigilance." And Mark 13:37 says "And what I say to you I say to all, stay awake." We must be awake to these things happening and do what we can to combat them in every way we can. But like with most things, awareness holds power. Because with that awareness, we can learn to adapt to what we face.

It turns out, one of the main causes for pollution in the water and the air is the stuff they are deliberately spraying in our skies and the pesticides they are cultivating our food with. Droughts are being engineered the same way floodings are. Unusual cold fronts, extreme weather changes, strong winds out of nowhere, destructive hurricanes, powerful tornadoes, unusual flooding, higher amounts of lightning during thunderstorms and even heat waves with extreme heat and low humidity can be attributed to these geoengineering activities. Even foggy evenings/mornings are the result due to their sun dimming practices. But no one wants to look to the obvious and instead everyone just wants to assume it's natural because of climate change.

This push for naming the cause for these things as "Climate Change" is all part of the plan. Because they want us to believe that overpopulation is causing an excessive increase in Carbon Dioxide which so happens to be allegedly damaging the "ozone layer" around the planet. But every high school freshman remembers basic Biology on how plants need and take in Carbon Dioxide and release Oxygen. Humans and animals need and take in Oxygen and release Carbon Dioxide. It's a variation of the circle of life in which our byproducts are what plants need to survive, and their byproducts are what we need to survive. This balance beautifully illustrates God's wisdom, omnipotence, and foresight, where He designed a system to keep equilibrium and balance at the heart of this place we inhabit.

But in order to help usher in an agenda, they want us to believe that there are too many people and animals on the planet and excess carbon emissions are contributing to this change in climate that will result in catastrophe if no action is taken. It's all about control. This belief that there's too many people on the planet warrants in their mind that the herd needs to be trimmed down to maintain control. But they can't flat out say it or act on it. So, they disguise their intentions with noble objectives and virtuous goals.

But this agenda is not new. These alarmists pushed for it in the 80's stating that by the year 2000, "Entire nations could be wiped off the face of the Earth by rising sea levels if the global warming trend was not reversed." They pushed again in the early 2000's with the Kyoto Protocol and then with Al Gore's "An Inconvenient Truth." The idea then and even now is that climate change is happening at an alarming rate and if nothing is done, the world will end before our children's children have had a chance at it.

But what if climate change was really happening because of this "Spraying of the Skies" and the way weather is now being weaponized? That would be the perfect "Problem-Reaction-Solution cycle we keep seeing not only here but in other areas of society.

Dr. Judith Curry is a climatologist and has published over 140 scientific books. She states that climate change in the manner we are told about is not accurate and has an agenda behind it. However, the media completely ignores her claims. Professor Ian Pilmer has studied the changes in climate and agrees with Dr. Curry. The founder of Weather Action, Piers Corby states that $CO_2$ has no effect on climate change, contrary to what they want us to believe. John Coleman, the founder of The Weather Channel also says there is no global warming. But then we have Greta Thunberg who was 16 years old at the time, speaking at the UN's Climate Action Summit to world leaders. And all eyes and ears were on her. Yet she was not a scientist, had no formal education in regard to weather patterns and history, and was reading from a script. But the non-stop media coverage on her at the time over this topic was so vast, even now she is revered as the climate change spokesperson.

Her emotional appeal to world leaders urging them to do something for her future garnered media attention like no other. That's what media manipulation looks like. They find voices that align with a narrative and push them relentlessly from a bunch of angles in hopes that non-conforming voices get drowned out and eventually forgotten.

This change in the climate is not because of cows or people populating the Earth, or even because of gasoline cars and trucks driving on the highways. Climate change may very well be real, but the causes may be far more complex and controlled than we have been led to believe. While mainstream discourse attributes climate change largely to carbon emissions and industrial activity, mounting evidence and observable phenomena demand that we broaden the scope of inquiry.

We are living at a time where weather is now being weaponized and labeled as climate change to further an agenda that does not have our best interest in mind. Real people are being affected by this weaponized weather, and it seems like things are only getting worse.

The hundreds of patents on Cloud Seeding, Geoengineering, and Weather Modification show that real climate change is being affected at least in part if not all, by these man-made methods and experiments happening in our skies. Once we start paying attention to these artificial cloud formations and then seeing how the weather is being affected soon after the spraying occurs, then we can start connecting the dots more easily. It is only then that a full realization of how the skies are being manipulated, and weather is being used as a weapon. And this has been at play for quite some time.

## Chapter 18 – Vaccines

*"We're in the middle of an unregulated chemical experiment on our children and grandchildren, and we don't yet know the full consequences." -Dr. Pete Meyers*

Dresden James said recently that "When a well-packaged web of lies has been sold gradually to the masses over generations, the truth will seem utterly preposterous and it's speaker will be considered a raving lunatic." Here is one of those well-packaged lies: Vaccines helped to eradicate diseases and are a necessity for a healthy and thriving community. This is far from true, but to the masses, this is not even close to being up for debate.

Most people are under the impression that vaccines actually stopped diseases right in their tracks. But the reality is that most diseases radically declined before any vaccine was ever introduced. Scientific literature now admits this through graphs and published articles that illustrate when the disease began to appear, the steady decline of cases of that disease, and then the introduction of a vaccine. In 99.99% of the cases, the disease reached a peak and then began to steadily decline.

For example, in 1900, the number of people who died from Measles was 13.3 in 100,000. In 1940 that number dropped to .5 in 100,000. In 1960, the mortality rate was .02 in 100,000. The Measles vaccine wasn't introduced until 1963, which by then, the number was already drastically low. The same thing happened with Diphtheria, Typhoid, and Whooping Cough. By the time a vaccine was produced, the rate of death had dramatically fallen to almost nonexistent. In almost all cases, by the time a vaccine was ever created for a particular disease, that disease was already on the verge of being eradicated naturally. But the experts went on to give all the credit to the eradication of those diseases to vaccines. This idea was repeated so much that it became truth in the eyes of society.

The truth is, better nutrition, cleaner water, better sanitation practices, banned pesticides like DDT, and Immune System cellular memory passed down from our ancestors all helped curb severity and mortality from these illnesses that vaccines supposedly saved us from. This isn't to minimize the very real cases where children catch and suffer from Measles or other contagious illnesses. However, exposure to these diseases does help create a more robust immune system that is better able to deal with pathogens all throughout one's life. Natural Immunity will always exceed that of vaccine-induced Immunity. God designed it that way, on purpose.

Our Immune Systems were created with the purpose of getting stronger with use. Exposure to pathogens creates a stimulus' which strengthens our Immune Systems and creates lasting immunity. Memory of that immunity is imprinted on those Immune Cells and that memory gets passed on to every Immune Cell that comes after it. So, every generation of Immune cells that comes after the infection is that much more capable of dealing with future infections. This is because of what the older generations of immune cells had to overcome. That's in essence of how God created our Immune Systems to work. Much like a muscle, the more it's forced to strengthen and adapt, the more able it is to generate power. The more it's used, the stronger it gets. That's how our Immune Systems work as well.

When a baby is born, they are born with an Immune System, which is like hardware on a computer. That hardware is then programmed with software and part of that software for programming the Immune System is picking up illnesses during childhood. Children should get be getting sick, not avoiding it. Because those infections act as software updates that keep the hardware running at the optimal level it was designed to. Those early infections and allowing the body to adapt naturally prevent and protect against Cancer, Heart Disease, and so many other infections later in life.

There has to be a revolution when it comes to allopathic medicine because the medical profession has been completely controlled by Big Pharma, and root causes of disease are not being addressed. Symptom suppressing medication is only masking the symptoms but are not solving the problem. If anything, they're suppressing the body's ability to learn to fight off infections effectively and efficiently.

It turns out, most pediatrician's offices live off the income and benefits they get from administering vaccines. They are incentivized by vaccine manufacturers to have a high percentage of their patients vaccinated. And their practice could not be sustained without these incentives. In fact, many would be out of business rather quickly. It is a vaccine enterprise market and offices that don't push for and have enough kids getting vaccinated, will not have the monetary incentives to keep them in business.

These incentives not only come from the vaccine manufacturers but also from insurance companies. Small doctor's offices can easily be very profitable if they comply. These offices are even given classes that show them and their staff how to communicate more effectively to better get parents to comply and follow the vaccine schedule. They are taught how to subtly gaslight, shame, threaten, and coerce parents to get compliance. Because they know that if they don't, their offices won't be around to survive for long.

Vaccine inserts are papers folded in every which way so that they can inconspicuously fit inside the box of where a vaccine came in. They're rarely read by doctors and even more rarely seen by parents. But they have a myriad of information, most of which seems overly complicated so that no one looks too much into them. Health professionals just trust what they are told by the drug companies and pharmaceutical reps that market and sell them. But if one was to look at the ingredients of all these vaccines on those inserts, and research what they do and how they affect living tissue, they'd never vaccinate again.

Even the slightest bit of research would lend itself to the discovery of what is really in these things. And that research would lend itself to an awareness that many of the ingredients in and of themselves are actually harmful and toxic to human health. So much so that it would be hard to imagine anyone believing that being injected with any of these toxic ingredients, much less any combination of them, would improve their health and save their lives.

For example, the vaccine insert for just the MMR vaccine contains 42 paragraphs of warnings and adverse reactions.

Warnings that if anybody took the time to look through and actually read, would think twice about giving it to their child. One of the side effects is the actual disease that the vaccine is supposed to protect against, which is Measles. Other side effects noted include seizures, encephalitis, pneumonia, and even death. And Section 13.1 of every FDA approved insert has this: "This vaccine has not been tested for carcinogenesis or mutagenesis..." This translates to, they don't know the long-term effects that injecting this into the body might have. It can cause mutations that lead to cancer or may cause cancer just with the ingredients by themselves.

Just by reading a package insert inside the box that a vaccine comes in, any parent will have more information than the actual doctor administering the vaccines. And with that information, one can make a better-informed decision.

In 1962, the amount of vaccines required for children was only five doses. By 1983, that number had increased to 24 doses. In 1986, the National Childhood Vaccine Injury Act (NCVIA) was established as a way to shield vaccine manufacturers from liability for injuries caused by vaccines. On paper, the goal was to ensure a stable vaccine supply and prevent lawsuits from deterring vaccine development. Under this Act, individuals harmed by vaccines would be able to seek compensation through the National Vaccine Injury Compensation Program (VICP) and not sue the vaccine manufacturers directly. This would shift the financial burden of payouts to taxpayers and remove any liability from the drug companies. That convenience would now allow these vaccine makers to make a product that could cause bodily harm and they would not be liable for it.

Countless injuries have been occurring since then, but because of this act and media blackout on these injuries, the general public remains unaware. Even today, just applying and getting accepted to get a payout based on an injury obviously caused by a vaccine has proven to be extremely difficult and tedious with many hoops and barriers to cross. It's estimated that more than 75% of the people that apply for this are denied, keeping the numbers skewed and under-reported. This makes it seem like there aren't as many injuries from vaccines than there actually is, giving a false sense of safety.

As soon as this act was passed into law in 1986, the amount of vaccines recommended for children jumped even higher. In 2016, the amount of vaccines was up to 72 doses and today it is at 108 and climbing. If a child gets all the vaccines on today's schedule, they'll get almost 13,000 micrograms of Aluminum, 600 micrograms of Mercury, and over 200 different chemicals. These are all toxins that can't just be thrown out in the trash but rather someone in a hazmat suit needs to remove them carefully and dispose of them properly. But health professionals and parents are fine with putting them inside children with the false promise that they will prevent diseases.

Even with that in mind, they want us to believe that there's nothing to see here. Except Autism has gone from 1 in 150 to 1 in 36 today. And for boys, the rates are even higher. 1 in every 22 boys has Autism today. But when researcher Dan Olmsted looked into the Amish, who don't vaccinate their children, he found only 3 cases of Autism.

And those 3 cases were children who had been adopted after they were vaccinated.

In general, Autism just doesn't exist in the Amish. And when Dr. James Neuenschwander did a study, he found that the more vaccine visits a child is subjected to, the more likely it is that the child will develop Autism. Just 1 vaccine visit increased the risk of Autism by 70%. If a child did every visit that the vaccine schedule recommended, the risk went up to 440%.

The argument being used to combat these stats is based on a fallacy easily disproven. They say it's because of procedures in place for "better diagnosis" or an "increased awareness." But we don't see 1 in 36 adults with Autism over the age of 50 or 1 in 22 elderly males in nursing homes. If all it takes to increase the rate of Autism is better diagnosis" it would be true of every age group and not just the ones born after 1985.

Since 1990, ADHD has increased by 819%, Bipolar in youth has increased by 10,833%, Chronic Fatigue Syndrome has increased by 11,027% and allergies have risen by more than 50%. Today, 1 in 12 kids have food allergies. 1 in 5 have chronic illnesses. And 1 in 285 will be diagnosed with cancer before their 20$^{th}$ birthday. It's not to say that vaccines are causing all of this but there is a cumulative effect that has been going on for some time. And the combination of things are wreaking havoc mostly on our youth.

If you were to give your child the ingredients in a vaccine to eat, you'd be charged with a crime. But injecting them into your children at a doctor's office and it's now called healthcare.

Since 1989, over $5 Billion has been paid out to vaccine injury and death victims through the National Vaccine Injury Compensation Program. Imagine what that number would be if the approval rate for claims was higher than the 25%, where it's currently at. Or if more primary care physicians would actually document the cases and not block them from progressing through as vaccine induced injuries. Or if the vaccine manufacturers actually had to pay out of pocket for those injuries instead of the government/taxpayers footing the bill.

If vaccines were truly safe and effective for everyone like they want us to believe, why does this fund even exist? And why are the doctors that actually looked into the Science behind vaccines and have been very vocal about the side effects being silenced. And why do we continue to see childhood health plummeting since 1990 and continues to do so.

Vaccines were introduced under the premise that they would create beneficial health outcomes that would far outweigh the risks. But the truth was far from it. In fact, not one of the 43 vaccines mandated for children has ever been tested for safety in a placebo-controlled trial. Health & Human Services or HHS has admitted this, though that paperwork is hard to find on the HHS website. And the "so called" diseases that vaccines prevent you from getting are not diseases but rather illnesses. They are things our fathers and forefathers dealt with and overcame. They were not life threatening, but rather just annoying.

Obviously, no one wants their child sick but it is an important part of developing and strengthening that innate Immune System that God endowed us with. Like it was stated earlier, immune systems are one of those things that get stronger with use. The repeated exposure to germs and pathogens forces it to become more efficient and effective at overcoming illnesses. This allows the body to build a faster and more targeted defense over time. Illnesses, while often seen as harmful, play a crucial role in this process. They train the Immune System to distinguish between harmful and harmless agents, ultimately making it more resilient and responsive. That's how God created this system to work, and it's on us to trust the system and to trust God.

Fear and propaganda are powerful tools used to manipulate public perception about illnesses and disease. This often pushes people toward decisions that serve others' interests rather than their own. By flooding media with emotionally charged messages and selective information, those in power can override people's critical thinking and create a false sense of urgency or consensus. And in essence, can cause doubt in God and the systems He put into place. That doubt tends to grow and fester.

In 1 Corinthians 6:19-20, it says "Do you not know that your bodies are temples of the Holy Spirit, who is in you, whom you have received from God? You are not your own; you were bought at a price. Therefore honor God with your bodies." As it's been stated earlier, Satan cannot kill God. So, he will do whatever he can to hurt Him. One way he can do that is through defiling the temple that is our bodies. Because of this, we must be mindful of what we put into our bodies and what we put on them.

Keeping the temple clean, pure, and unpolluted should be one of our highest priorities and one we need to attend to daily. Through deceitfulness, perversion and long-game tactics, Satan has found ways to taint, corrupt and defile that temple that is our bodies through various ways. One of the more significant ways is through contaminating it with cells from an aborted fetus. The killing of babies, whether born or unborn is Satan's ultimate way of bringing pain to God. And so, when cells of those babies that were murdered, are injected into healthy humans, voluntarily, it's Satan's way of sending a message to God.

No one would voluntarily inject themselves or their children with aborted baby cells. So pharmaceutical companies use terms like WI-38 and MRC-5 to mask the ingredients that are from the aborted fetal cells used in many of the vaccines today. They use these terms to deflect from where these cells really come from. But because most people won't ever look too much into it, or research for themselves, these ingredients are never questioned.

But a simple search would tell you that WI-38 are cells from the lung tissue of a 3-month-old female fetus that was electively aborted. MRC-5 are cells from the lung tissue of a 14 week-old male fetus, which was also electively aborted. And like it was mentioned earlier, one of the more profound ways that Satan can hurt God is through the killing of innocent babies. But if he can convince a whole group of people that the killing of babies is their right, or even a necessity, and then to use cells from the death of those babies to inject into the masses, is an ultimate disrespect.

And because these aborted cell lines are coming from a male and a female fetus, they have DNA that corresponds to the sex they were before they were aborted. When male DNA is injected into females, it can cause all types of issues that are not readily visible or apparent right away. And the same thing happens when female DNA is injected in males. The fact that these cell lines are used in various vaccines, and those various vaccines are injected numerous times into these children should be a cause for concern.

Other ingredients included in vaccines that most of the general public is unaware of are kidney cells from a monkey, kidney cells from a dog, and fetal cow serum which is obtained from the blood of cow fetuses. They use initials and jargon to make these ingredients seem less dramatic than they really are.

For example, the kidney cells from a dog are labeled as MDCK which stands for Madin-Darby Canine Kidney cells. That's just a fancy way of saying they're cells from a Cocker Spaniel puppy. On paper, they use these cells because they provide a reliable, long-lasting, and stable environment for growing viruses that are needed to create certain vaccines.

A more nefarious reason they use DNA from the cells of other humans and species is to trigger an autoimmune reaction. The problem is, autoimmune reactions come with their own set of problems, that usually linger and last a lifetime. Think of it this way. When a person gets an organ transplant, they are prescribed certain drugs that they will have to take for the rest of their lives. These drugs are called anti-rejection drugs and are designed to lower your Immune System's reaction to these foreign organs and cells. Your Immune System automatically knows that these cells/tissues you are obtaining through donation are not yours and will immediately seek to destroy these cells/tissues. The body will reject and destroy any tissue that is foreign, because it recognizes that these cells/tissue are not carrying your DNA. It's a great system made by God but a tricky one if you're in need of a transplant. Or if you're injecting foreign DNA into your body.

So now, Cocker Spaniel DNA coupled with other types of cells from other types of organisms are mixed with chemicals and injected into newborns and toddlers. It's no wonder autoimmune diseases are on the rise. And immunity seems to be on the decline. The body is constantly attacking itself and because it's so busy attacking itself, its resources for attacking foreign invaders and pathogens is low.

So, are vaccines really necessary for health and longevity? The research shows unvaccinated people are among the healthiest compared to the vaccinated. One cohort study looked at individuals born in the 1950's, before vaccine schedules were created, and looked at their general health today. The difference was night and day. Five other separate studies now show that "if children go natural, no vaccines whatsoever, they too have the best outcomes."

There are over 200 published studies showing how vaccines cause an immune system dysregulation. This means their immune systems are not as effective as they're supposed to be and in turn they tend to get sick more often.

A study done from 1980 to 2001 by the NIH, The National Institute of Health, found that for 20 years, the percentage of seniors getting flu shots increased sharply from 15% to 65%. It would stand to reason that Flu deaths among the elderly should've taken a dramatic drop. Instead, Flu deaths among the elderly continued to climb, which left researchers dumbfounded.

So, they crunched the numbers, adjusted for every possible factor and still found no reduction in Flu deaths. They then went on to look at other countries and found the same was true there as well. The conclusion: Flu shots did not reduce Flu deaths among the elderly. In fact, many believe they actually contributed to them.

Another study that was just released from the Cleveland Clinic looked at the effectiveness of the Flu shot today and showed that this year's Flu shots led to a 27% higher risk of getting the Flu. That means you were more likely to get the Flu if you were vaccinated against it, which in turn, signifies those who are not vaccinated may already have protection against it.

As you can imagine, these studies garnered very little attention and never reached the masses. They would've pierced through the narrative and caused many to question whether vaccines were even slightly effective.

More studies are starting to come out that show how vaccines don't just affect our immune systems but also affect our brains and bodies as well. Aluminum and Mercury are just 2 of the many toxins that are able to punch through the Blood-Brain Barrier, causing Encephalitis or brain inflammation, neurological disorders, distress in our Nervous System, and even death. That's where SIDS or Sudden Infant Death comes in. Upon investigations, it was observed that these incidents usually occurred around the same time that vaccine visits to the doctor happened.

Sudden Infant Death Syndrome is the "unexplained" death of an apparently healthy baby during sleep. These instances surged the late 80s and early 90s and had parents, doctors, and healthcare professionals baffled but grasping for answers. They started looking at cribs, the bedding, and even the parents.

It wasn't until 2021 where a peer-reviewed study in Toxicology Reports revealed what many had long suspected. This study looked at over 2600 infant deaths reported to VAERS and found that 58% occurred within 3 days of vaccination. And 78.3% occurred within 7 days.

A separate internal report from Glaxo Smith Kline, a multinational pharmaceutical company, revealed during a court case in Italy that 97% of post-vaccine infant deaths occurred within 10 of vaccination. Even after this, public health officials often dismiss such cases as unexplained. The dots are never connected because the dots are never to be looked at.

Experts tend to find what they look for and if they don't look, they'll rarely find. When something doesn't fit into the current framework, it often goes unseen or unstudied. Not because nothing was there, but because they weren't willing to look for it. That's how the Science around vaccines works.

For those who have eyes to see and ears to hear, the research is becoming more clear. Unvaccinated children are far healthier than their counterparts and vaccines do cause more harm than many of us have been led to believe. Injury from vaccines aren't so rare and they are not "safe and effective" like they keep parroting. We've just been programmed to believe that autoimmune disorders, ear infections, sinus infections, allergies, Eczema, seizures, and SIDS are all normal.

It's hard to imagine believing the human body was designed so poorly, so innately broken and weak that in order to maintain health, brand new babies need 25 plus injections of man-made concoctions filled with synthetic chemicals, heavy metals, animal secretions, and aborted fetal cells before they even turn one. All in the name of trusting the Science to keep them healthy.

And how does it make sense to inject our live children with little bits and pieces of dead children through these aborted fetal cells? How does any thinking person assume that health, vitality, or life can come from an industry rooted in and made possible by the perpetuation of chronically ill people. It is not in their interest to have healthy humans because that means less of a customer base.

At the end of the day, it's not so much about being "anti-vaccine" but rather being pro-truth and pro-Science. The very notion that injecting foreign agents, metals, biologicals, and toxins into the body can improve health and prevent disease is not just delusional but a blasphemous defiance of the divine order.

Our babies were not born with a pharmaceutical deficiency. They don't need a shot full of Aluminum, formaldehyde, and aborted fetal cells to achieve health. Somewhere along the line, a mass disconnect occurred and now people refuse to look into what they inject into their children and themselves. They'd much rather blindly trust the experts because that's what they've been conditioned to do. But some are starting to awaken from their slumber. They're starting to see the future costs of their present decisions and recognize that consequences can have a lasting impact.

# Chapter 19 – Covid

*"Science used to be a systematic approach of continual questioning, experimentation, and discovery. It is now an infallible corporate-backed dogma that only selectively ordained "experts" are allowed to know or speak of."* -Alex Zeck

When Covid hit the scene, the level of conditioning ran rampant. The "powers that be" tied every virtue they could to compliance, behavioral and social rewards and punishments. People believed that them being compliant made them more intelligent and better than someone that didn't comply. That complicity would come at a cost that is now becoming evident to those who pay attention. But just like magicians who rely on sleight of hand and distraction to control where the audience looks, so too has the media.

And so, many remain unaware of the ramifications of their decision and attribute the complications they're experiencing or seeing others experience to random events or just a part of life. But our bodies were not made to be so innately delicate and unadaptable that diseases that normally only affect older people randomly start affecting the youth in outrageous numbers.

Corporations made billions, while the manufacturers were shielded from liability. The agencies that were supposed to look out for the people ignored the signals while the media colluded with "fact-checkers" to smear all dissent. Psychologists crafted the message while the propagandists charted the slogans. And everyday normal people were terrorized, isolated, and gaslit into submission. The idea was not about saving lives but rather about control. Daily death counts became a grim fixture on television news broadcasts. Networks displayed these numbers prominently, often in real-time tickers, emphasizing this need for fear and panic.

The constant updates served as a sobering reminder that not everything was as it seemed. And the goal was to shape and reinforce public perception around fear, panic, and distress. They were beta testing the use of mass hypnotic fear to control people and guide them in the direction of their choosing. And it worked on so many.

"Do Not Fear" is listed in the Bible 365 times. And when something is listed as a "do not…" it's likened to a command, a directive, a demand. It's specifically telling you not to do something. And the fact that it's in the Bible so many times, maybe God knew this would be one of the things that we struggled with the most. And how it could and would easily be used against us, to control us, and even defeat us, if we allowed it to.

So how come so many people were dying? And how come everyone who died of COVID, died at the hospital? No one was actually dying of COVID at their house. That should've been the first major red flag that at least deserved some looking into. Especially since "adverse effects from medical treatment", is the third leading cause of death in the U.S. This adverse effect from medical treatment is called Iatrogenic Illness and refers to any injury or sickness caused by doctor error, hospital error, or healthcare interventions that result in the death of the patient. It's a pretty significant thing here in the U.S. But because this rarely gets any media attention, most people remain unaware of how common it has become. The fact that it is now the 3rd leading cause of death is pretty significant, even with little to no media attention.

When COVID was running rampant, one of the main protocols that was pushed insistently in every hospital in the US was a medication called Remdesivir plus the use of ventilators. In 2018, Remdesivir was too unethical to put into Ebola clinical trials in Africa because it had a 53% kill rate. Ebola doesn't even have a 53% kill rate. All the nurses and hospital staff knew Remdesivir as "Run, Death Is Near" because it was notorious for causing organ failure in the patients.

And the ventilators were known for triggering deadly Pneumonia which exacerbated their breathing difficulties. Even though the staff knew these things, they were instructed to continue following this protocol. Later, a study conducted by a team at Northwestern University uncovered this pattern, and it shattered the official narrative.

But because it was not aligned with the narrative in place, legacy media gave it no airtime and fact-checkers continued dismissing these claims. And to the masses, if it didn't come out on the news on TV, then it's not reliable, factual information. So, many remained unaware of what really killed their family members.

There has been an explosion of cancer in those who got the mRNA vaccines. People from all ages, some that were in remission from a previous cancer or others who never had cancer to begin with, are suddenly being diagnosed. And for the first time in history, something called "Turbo

Cancer" is popping up everywhere. This is where cancer appears in the body and in just a few months has spread so violently all over the body, that metastasis overwhelms the organ systems. Traditional means to combat this type of cancer are usually ineffective. And now the scientific literature is showing that the mRNA therapy was actually producing spike proteins that were binding to DNA, and in turn making those cells abnormal. Then every time those affected cells would replicate, cancer would arise.

At any given moment, there are numerous cancer cells throughout our bodies. But our innate Immune Systems are designed to eliminate those cancerous cells with ease. But for some reason, those who got the mRNA injection are having trouble suppressing the cancers. The doors to allowing the Immune System to go in there and correct the problems are shut, stopping our God-given systems that are in place to fix such issues.

Some studies are now showing synthetic DNA contaminants are being found in the mRNA vials. Even before this study, some experts were sounding the alarm about the potential of mRNA being able to be reverse transcribed into the DNA of our cells, which is a real possibility.

The fact-checkers went on the offensive with labels for every post and disinformation articles that worked to at least muddy the waters and quell dissent. But these new studies were showing actual DNA in some of the vials, which meant people were being injected DNA into their bodies and were never made aware of this. This was not initially disclosed and even now has not been completely admitted to.

But when the potential for this to be a problem was first made clear, it was argued against full on by the experts. People were gaslit and claims were quickly dismissed. Because they knew that if the general public was ever made aware of how this technology could infiltrate cells and change their genomes, GMO would take on a whole new meaning.

The technology in the mRNA injections are also now proving to be something called "self-replicating." This means that they can replicate by themselves, autonomously inside the bodies of those injected, forever. And with that autonomous replication, the spreading from one person to another is amplified, similar to what we know as shedding.

In the simplest terms, shedding is when a vaccinated individual releases or sheds the components of the vaccine onto the people around them. The theory holds that they can vaccinate everyone without actually needing to vaccinate everyone individually. This not only violates "Informed Consent" laws but also poses some great concerns to those who do not wish to vaccinate.

Blood clots are also on the rise. Doctors who perform autopsies and funeral directors that embalm bodies are now seeing these unusual blood clots were never seen before the pandemic. These blood clots are long and fibrous with elastic qualities and tend to resemble rubber bands, or even calamari. They are large white fibrin structures and contain no properties of blood.

These clots are being found blocking arteries, cutting off circulation to extremities, and obstructing organs from getting blood supply. It turns out, the spike protein that was supposed to stay in the localized area of the injection site was invading the brain, the heart, the bone marrow, and the Immune System. It's been found that it's not only playing a role in this rise of all types of cancer but also in the formation of these blood clots that are popping up in the vaccinated. This is causing some scientists to even call these abnormal clots "engineered biostructures."

Medicare has shelled out over 6 billion dollars for Xarelto and over 16 billion for Eliquis, both of which are blood clot medications designed to treat these types of conditions. The amount of money that could be saved by getting to the root cause of the issues and tackling it there is pretty significant.

But because of the way the medical industry complex is set up, no one is connecting the dots as to why and where these symptoms and diseases are coming from. They just continue reacting, dumbfounded by the rise in disease and death all over the world. It's as if there's nothing to see here, even if all the clues point to where they don't want to look.

Another consequence of the mRNA vaccine technology is being seen with athletes from all arenas, even at the high school level. The surge in sudden deaths due to heart-related incidents has been climbing exponentially since the start of the pandemic. Myocarditis, which is the inflammation of the heart walls, is on the rise, leading to heart conditions that have never been seen at the level they are now being seen. Sudden deaths among athletes has increased 1700% just between 2021 and 2022. Pericarditis is up 690%, Myocarditis is up 610%, and Guilian-Barre Syndrome is up by 250%.

If one of Satan's goals was to infiltrate medicine to create a frail, feeble, and sickly people, under the guise that it was helping them, he may have succeeded to a certain extent. Because never in recent history have we seen the rate of illness and disease that we are seeing now. Sudden Adult Death Syndrome or SADS is now a thing. And just like with SIDS, which is Sudden Infant Death Syndrome, no one can understand why adults and young people are dying suddenly, out of the blue.

A massive study of 99 million people who received the Covid Vaccine was published and the article headline says it all. "Largest Vaccine Study Ever Finds Shots Are Linked to Small Increased Risks of Neurological Blood & Heart Disorders – But They Are Still Extremely Rare." Every statement about the study went out of its way to describe the injuries as rare. But what exactly does "rare" actually mean?

In terms of this study, rare means a 3.18 times risk of swelling of the brain and spinal cord. This means you are increasing your risk of brain and spinal swelling by 318% over someone who didn't get the vaccine. There was also a 2.86 times risk of Guillan-Barre Syndrome, which is a form of paralysis. People were 286% more likely to suffer from this over someone that never got the vaccine. The risk of Myocarditis was 6.10 and Pericarditis was 6.91. These conditions affect the walls of the heart and many believe they are irreversible. If each of these potential injuries are so rare like the article would like you to believe, are they still rare when you add them altogether?

Take the Moderna Vaccine for example. Using the standard 3 shot schedule, a person would be increasing their risk of brain and spinal swelling by 378% with the first shot, but also adding a 348% risk of Myocarditis with that same first shot. A 610% increase in Myocarditis with the 2$^{nd}$ shot and another 201% increase of Myocarditis with the 3$^{rd}$ shot.

And these are just the adverse events that the study looked at. All of a sudden rare doesn't seem so rare, especially for the millions of people that have been affected or have a loved one affected.

The American Diabetes Association admits that 40% of all Covid deaths were Diabetics. This organization has been around since 1939 and their mission statement is to prevent and cure Diabetes and to improve the lives of all people affected by Diabetes. In 1980, there were over 5 million Americans with Diabetes. In 2010, it was over 21 million Americans. In 2023 it was up to 38 million.

An organization that for more than 84 years committed to curing and preventing Diabetes seems to not be making any headway towards their goal. The same thing can be said with all these other associations and organizations. Despite their mission statements and goals, what does their progress towards those goals look like? Yes they may raise money, host 5K walks, and have their banners and billboards posted everywhere, but where are the results? In Matthew 21:19, Jesus saw a fig tree full of leaves but with no fruit. *"He said to it, 'May you never bear fruit again!' Immediately the tree withered"*. The tree had the appearance of life and promise, yet it produced nothing of real value. This shows that looking productive without producing results is unacceptable. Appearance alone is meaningless if there is no actual productivity.

At this point we need some clarification on the difference between Science and scientists. Because we are living in a time when people keep saying they trust the Science, but never really go and look at what the Science actually says. They are only looking at the scientists and how they trust them with their interpretation of the information. But real Science is the study of observable and measurable things.

Science is about questioning and never being satisfied with the answers. Science is dynamic, always changing, and is never settled. Science is pure and cannot be corrupted by influence, such as money, power, or human motivation. Scientists however, are people that CAN be corrupted. Many of them have degrees and as part of their training, they may have memorized information from textbooks and lectures in an effort to pass the course.

So when people say they believe in vaccines because they believe the Science, one has to wonder if they actually read the research? Do they understand the Scientific Method? Or are they confused between believing the Science and believing the scientists? Scientists are human, which means they are vulnerable to all of the same temptations that lead other humans to engage in practices that are less than pure or honest. Those temptations include the promise of money, power, control, and prestige.

And while these scientists and doctors may start out with excellent and pure intentions, all humans are subject to finding themselves in situations where they may be pressured to sacrifice the truth for the sake of their careers, lifestyles, and legacies.

Science, on the other hand, is not subject to any of those human temptations. The doctors and scientists who do support vaccination generally work for the Centers Disease Control, World Health Organization, American Academy of Pediatrics, American Medical Association, and the vaccine manufacturers. All of these scientists are people that have built their lives and their lifestyles on the expectation that they will be reimbursed for supporting and promoting the belief that vaccines are both safe and effective.

They are incentivized to support skewed findings that benefit the agenda of the corporations they work for. Corporations that regularly sacrifice the truth in the interest of maintaining their own goals and visions. That's when "the Science" becomes corrupt. That's when it becomes less about the Science, and more about the scientists and the machines they work for.

So, when it comes to the health and the very lives of our children, we need to get back to Science and stop putting our trust in these scientists. Because currently, the real Science does not support vaccination as a practice that increases health or wellness. In fact, it shows the opposite. One only has to scratch the surface, and all things begin to be revealed.

For example, every drug that has been recalled by the FDA was first proven to be "safe and effective." So, to think that these "for profit" drug companies have our best interest in mind is how Satan has deceived the masses. Revelation 18:23 tells us "...for by their sorceries were all nations deceived." In Greek, the word "sorceries" is "pharmakeia", which can mean witchcraft, magic arts, or pharmaceuticals. So at least questioning and investigating should be a starting point.

This idea of questioning and looking into the most historically corrupt and fraudulent companies and entities in the world does not make you "anti" anything. Nor does it make you a conspiracy theorist. Actually, questioning is and should be the place of reason. The fact that questioning has become taboo and is often met with ridicule or dismissal rather than thoughtful engagement should raise concerns. This shift has discouraged open dialogue and critical thinking, replacing curiosity with conformity. But questioning is the foundation of reason. It challenges assumptions, helps reveal blind spots, and fuels progress.

Instead of silencing questions, we should create space for them. Because truth doesn't fear inquiry but lies always do. And the Father of Lies, who is Satan, wants to hurt God in any and every way he can. And he will continue doing it though medicine and medical technologies. It's on us question, investigate, and use discernment.

# Chapter 20 - The Earth

*"The Earth is what we all have in common."* – Wendell Berry

It's been said that it's easier to deceive a person than it is to convince them they've been deceived. The deception around where we truly live is deep and entangled with so many other things. The level of conditioning about this place we inhabit starts at the earliest of ages and through repetition, continually gets hammered into the subconscious.

This has been going on for generations and is now to the point that people never even question the shape of the Earth. They have become so deeply conditioned by this belief that they stop questioning it altogether. Over time, this has become their version of truth, so ingrained that any challenge to it feels like an attack. Ironically, the more false or fragile the belief, the more aggressively it's defended. If you dare to question it, you're not just wrong in their eyes, you're foolish, and even dangerous. That's the power of collective conditioning. It turns lies into "common sense" and dissent into heresy.

The hardest part of this coming age will be for those most educated to unlearn most of what they've been taught and to make space for the real truth to set in. It won't be about learning new truths. It will be about unlearning the old ones. So much of what people actually believe has been passed down, repeated, and reinforced until it feels absolute. But to see clearly and objectively, they'll need to tear down those mental walls and invisible barriers about what they believe. And mental walls are never built overnight. Most people don't even know the walls are there. They've decorated them, made homes inside them, and will fight tooth and nail to protect them. Not because the beliefs are true but because the walls feel safe. A lie repeated enough times becomes sacred. And anyone who questions it gets ridiculed. Not because they're wrong, but because they're threatening a comfortable illusion. Real truth requires space to settle in. And that space only opens up when we let go of what never belonged there in the first place.

If we don't really know for sure where we live and the shape of this place, then all sorts of other questions come into play. Questions like: Are we alone in the universe? Is there life on Mars? Are there Aliens? What is the actual age of this place? How did evolution come to be? What about the dinosaurs? And so on. So, to clear the air right away, let me start with this uncomfortable truth: the Earth is flat, it is non-rotating or stationary and is enclosed by some kind of solid structured dome known as the firmament. Inside the firmament is the sun, the moon, and the stars, all of which move about in predictable patterns in the sky. Above and below are waters. All of this is in the bible, we just happen to selectively overlook it.

In Genesis 1:6-7, it tells us "And God said, let there be a firmament in the midst of the waters and let it divide the waters from the waters. And God made the firmament and divided the waters which were under the firmament from the waters that were above the firmament, and it was so." Isaiah 40:22 says "It is God who sits above the circle of the Earth, and its inhabitants are like grasshoppers; it is He who stretches out the heavens like curtains and spreads them out like a tent to dwell in." Proverbs 8:27 states "When He prepared the heavens, I was there; when He drew a circle upon the face of the deep *and* stretched out the firmament over it."

Zechariah 1:11 talks about the Earth being stationary. It says " ...and behold, all the Earth sits at rest." In essence, the Earth is a circle (Isiah 40:22) made with a compass (proverbs 8:27), laid upon a face (Genesis 1:2), which is bound (Job 26:10) at its ends (Job 38:13). It does not move (Psalm 93:1) and is covered by a dome (Genesis 1:6-8), containing the sun, moon, and stars (Genesis 1:14-18), which are revolving around us (Enoch 75:3-4).

It must be made known that the Bible does reference Earth being shaped as a circle but it's important to note that a circle is not a sphere. The Earth in essence, is a horizontal, toroidal, energetic plane with a firmament above as a boundary and Antarctica acting as the perimeter, guarding the edge of our known realm.

The easiest way to describe the Earth is through the resemblance of a snow globe. A snow globe is a flat, circular area surrounded by half circle glass enclosing the environment within it. This is where we get the word hemisphere, which literally means half circle. So, the Earth is round, but not in the shape of a globe or sphere. It does have an invisible vaulted dome that acts just like the glass on the snow globe.

The Bible calls this dome the firmament, and it surrounds the Earth with the highest part of the dome being at the center, which is the North Pole. The Antarctic ice wall is what surrounds and holds everything in, acting as the perimeter. The most accurate description using a map is the Gleason's Map because it basically shows the true shape of the Earth. Ironically, this map is also used as the logo for United Nations.

Every single ancient culture depicted the firmament and the flat Earth. From the Greeks to the Egyptians to the Navajo to the Babylonians, to the Japanese, to the Persians, and even to the Mayans - they all knew the shape and structure of our world.

They say it's because of technology that we now know the true shape. But Universal Pictures began using the image of a rotating Earth 30 years before anyone had ever even seen it. At that point, no one had ever been high enough to get a true perspective of where we lived. But there it was, the symbolic sphere rotating on an axis, repeatedly showcased before every movie and show. They were conditioning the mind, repeatedly exposing it to specific patterns until recognition became automatic.

In 1931, a man by the name of Augustine Piccard traveled 51,000 feet into the upper atmosphere and was among the first persons to get a glimpse of what things really looked like from up there. Upon his return to land, he was quoted as saying "The Earth seemed like a flat disk with upturned edges." He is credited as being the first to ever reach those heights.

2 years later, Russian astronauts got up to 62,300 feet and said they were looking for some sort of curvature but could not find any. So, at this point, the eyewitness accounts were not aligning with the narrative and the goal

they had in mind. But they persisted with the training and conditioning of society.

Around 1947, the discovery of the ice wall in Antarctica led to what is now known as Operation High Jump. This was led by Admiral Richard Byrd in an attempt to map out the outer edges of our world. Known as one of the largest Antarctic expeditions ever, there were over 13 ships and 33 aircraft, some of which were lost after experimenting with the limits of the firmament.

In 1956, the discovery of the firmament led to Operation Deep Freeze. On paper, the main objectives were to establish a more permanent research station in Antarctica, to provide support to scientists doing research there, and to establish reliable supply chains.

In 1958, nuclear weapons were fired into the upper atmosphere to see what was there and how high it really was. By then it was obvious that there was an upper and outer firmament and that it was self-regenerating and impenetrable. Operation Paperclip was created as a result, utilizing Nasa and German scientists who specialized in rockets, aviation, chemical/biological warfare, and missile technology.

There was controversy because many if not all these German scientists were members of the Nazi party and worked on weapons used against civilians. But this was quickly overlooked since the end justified the means. And that end was to develop technology that would break through the firmament. Many of these scientists went on to work for NASA.

The Antarctic Treaty was established soon afterward as a means to guard the firmament and keep curious eyes and ears away from the area. Then a few years later, these same scientists along with our military were tasked with nuking the firmament with high altitude atomic bombs in what started out as Operation Fishbowl and then later termed Operation Dominic. The goal was to see how impenetrable that firmament really was.

Today, that firmament is held as a closely guarded truth amongst elites because they know that if the general public ever became truly aware, it would cause the house of cards to all fall down and the domino effect would have far reaching effects for all of humanity.

Any time Flat Earth is mentioned, the immediate and default thought is ridiculousness, laughable and even comical. "It's so obvious that the Earth is round and is spinning." But is it really obvious? Or are we just unconsciously fighting for the ideas that our captors have conditioned us with? We experience a flat Earth. We don't experience motion. Horizons are always flat, water always finds its level and all of human engineering doesn't compensate for curvature or spin. But everyone's unconscious response is, "it is obvious that world is a sphere."

I read about a professor who placed a diagram of a red circle and a blue circle on the display board and then asked his students which one is bigger. He started with the presupposition that even though it may seem like the circles were the same size, they in fact were not. One was bigger than the other and their task was to find out which one it was. At that point, some of the students started saying the red one was bigger, and others were saying that it was the blue one. After a few minutes of this ongoing debate, the professor stopped the exercise and went on to say that the circles really were the same size.

These students, before any information was provided to them, all believed that the circles were exactly the same size. But after they were fed information about them being different, they began to doubt what their eyes were telling them. They were forced to betray their instincts and what their senses were telling them because of what the authority at the time, which was their professor was telling them. Their senses had them believing the circles were the same size and all of them thought that initially. But because this authority, this expert in that arena told them that the circles were in fact not the same size even though they seemed like it, these students quickly betrayed their senses and instincts and rejected what their common sense told them. That's exactly how we have arrived here and how so many have been fooled and continued to be fooled.

From a very young age, kids are taught about the solar system and the characteristics of the planets. They are assigned Science projects over the Solar System and Science lessons on the Milky Way. They are taught about astronauts and the space shuttles they fly in. They are shown "rockets going into outer space" and videos of astronauts in "outer space." They are taught about the moon, the sun, and stars, and even shown pictures of the moon landing.

With all the same lies repeated over and over, kids are bombarded with theoretical information and so by the time they are at an age to think for themselves, they never even question the foundational "truths" they learned early on. They've been hammered with repetitious fallacies so consistently and congruently that the thought of any of that information being false seems outlandish. The training and conditioning is so systematic and strategic, that people will completely dismiss any evidence they are presented with. Their mind is made up and nothing will change it.

The frequency of these ideas hammered in with continual repetition since the earliest of ages has created somewhat of a religion in and of itself. That religion is called the Globocentrism which is a form of Spherianism, and anyone who questions it is labeled as a Flat Earther. As if that title has some sort of negative connotation attached to it. As if someone who questions the real shape of Earth is less intelligent, a non-thinker, and a mouth-breather. But critical thinking is the ability to objectively analyze information, question assumptions, and evaluate evidence before forming a conclusion. Regardless of whatever title they are given.

It goes beyond simply accepting what we're told. It requires curiosity, skepticism, and a willingness to consider multiple perspectives. In a world overloaded with misinformation and bias, critical thinking is essential for making informed decisions, solving complex problems, and protecting ourselves from manipulation. At its core, it empowers us to think for ourselves instead of being led by emotion, authority, or groupthink. It's about not trusting an expert's opinion on something but rather looking into it from all angles and seeing if it makes sense. The Earth being flat makes sense.

When it comes to outer space, it must be made clear that there is an upper atmosphere that is still under the firmament. And we do have technology that can take us up to this area, which is around 130,000 feet. At that altitude, it may appear and seem like outer space. In fact, most of the real images and video we see of outer space is taken from these heights. To give perspective, commercial aircraft travel at around 42,000 feet. Private jets can travel at slightly higher altitudes and military aircraft can travel up to 70,000 feet.

At these heights, the shape of Earth is easily evident and that is why many of the images from these altitudes come from a distorted lens known as a fish-eyed lens. This gives the appearance of the false shape of the Earth being what they claim; curved. Even the windows from the airplane are designed to distort what is seen through them giving the illusion of curvature. Supposedly it's not intentional but rather due to the curved window shape, but the deception still remains intact and congruent with the narrative they wish to maintain. But all types of clues and key features coupled with our experience living on this "planet" should already be telling us the truth.

No matter how high you ascend, the horizon will always remain level. Amateur weather balloon footage captures this level-ness all the time. That is because most amateurs tend to use regular camera lenses to be able to capture true images from "space" with no distortion. Most of the official footage that NASA releases however, is always taken using that fish-eyed lens, which distorts and creates the false curvature we keep seeing.

Fish-eye lenses are ultra-wide-angle lenses but because of that extreme angle, they tend to warp straight lines, especially near the edges. This creates those weird curved, convex, or concave effects that pop up when viewing video released from the experts. That's why it's important to pay attention because there are signs.

Perspective and how the human eyes work are based on our sense of spatial relationships and three-dimensionality. The further something gets away from us, the lower it's going to appear in our field of vision. Imagine a long straight road with streetlights that line it. If you are right under one of those lights, you have to look up to see it but the further the lights get, the lower they are going to appear in our field of vision.

That seems to explain what is happening with the moon and the sun. They are getting further away and so they are getting lower and lower in our field of vision. And at the end of this, it seems as if they vanish and we experience day turning to night. This is because light doesn't travel endlessly. We see this truth in the deep depths of the ocean. The further down you go, the more dark it becomes. At a certain point it will be so pitch black because of how deep you are that no matter how sunny it was on the surface of the water, that same light can only travel so far. This is why it seems like the sun disappears at night and reappears in the mornings. It has to do with how far it gets from the location we are at. But at the end of the day, both of these luminaries are still under the firmament. And they are still something God created to give light, mark time, and support life.

The Bible mentions the sun many times, often highlighting it as part of God's creation. For example, in Genesis 1:16, it says, "God made two great lights—the greater light to govern the day and the lesser light to govern the night." The "greater light" refers to the sun. The sun is also seen as a symbol of God's power and faithfulness. Psalm 19:4-6 describes the sun as a bridegroom coming out of his chamber, rejoicing to run its course across the sky. But yet they want us to believe the Sun is a massive ball of hot, glowing gases at the center of our solar system. And that it's 93 million miles away but even with that distance, it's still able to provide the light and heat necessary to sustain life, drive weather and ocean currents, and provide the necessary component that plants need to survive.

But the sun we experience is not 90 some million miles away. The very fact that localized light that is stemming from the sun proves that it's closer than they want us to believe. It's even been shown that clouds can sometimes be seen in front of and behind the sun, at the same time. This would be impossible if we were really barreling through space or if the sun was millions of miles away from the Earth. Time Zones also prove a sun that is closer than what they tell us. The local light given off from the sun works like a spotlight or flashlight from above. It doesn't light up the whole circle, but rather only a certain part of the circle. As the spotlight from above moves, it lights up one area while leaving another area dark, and this constant motion creates what we know as day and night. It also equates to the time differences we see in central standard time, eastern standard time and all the other time zones.

But if the moon was only illuminated because of the sun reflecting on it like the theory claims, why are there times when the sun and the moon can be seen at the same time. And what are the people on the other side of the world looking at if the moon is on this side during the day? And why does it look like grey "charcoal-like" dirt and craters in all the pictures and video of when they first "landed" on it? But when we look up to the moon, we see an illuminated surface as if the light is emanating from within the structure. And if it is 238,000 miles away, then why can we see so much detail on it?

We've been taught since elementary that the moon orbits around Earth, but the moon doesn't rotate the way we'd expect. It always shows us the same face. How is this possible if we are supposedly on a spinning ball zipping through space at over 1,000 miles per hour? Moonlight is also demonstrably cooler than moon shade, but sunlight does the opposite. And the fact that it moves in tight repetitive loops over a flat plane supports the flat Earth model.

We are told the circumference of the Earth is roughly 24,901 miles. That would mean that for every mile traveled, there would be 8 inches of curvature. That's just basic geometric math using the model of the Earth as a sphere like they keep telling us the Earth really is. If one were to convert those 8 inches into feet, it would be .666 feet. So aside from the irony that this number keeps popping up in this cosmological math they keep putting in our faces, this idea of curvature can easily be debunked. For example, the longest bridge in the world is the Danyang-Kunshan Grand Bridge and is over 102 miles long. Based on the math, there should be about 7,000 feet of dipping to account for curvature. But upon looking at it, even at just eye-level, the bridge is completely flat and straight. Whether you are using a really good zoom camera or you are seeing it from an aerial viewpoint, the bridge shows no sign of curvature even though the math and the Science say that there should be. And quite a bit of it.

Aircrafts and airplanes would also need to follow this compensation for curvature and adjust their flight path accordingly. Every mile traveled would require 8 inches of dipping the nose, just to prevent the plane from flying off into "space."

The SR-71 Blackbird is the world's fastest jet. It once set the record for flying from New York to London in 1 hour and 54 min. That's 3,459 miles and it did it in less than 2 hours. Because of the speeds that this jet was flying at, it would have to be dipping its nose 10 miles every minute just to keep it from flying off into "space." That type of effort and precision would have any pilot reeling and struggling to maintain their course. But looking at the flight path, it showed a straight direct path with no type of account for curvature.

The rail gun is a military weapon using a line-of-sight model to shoot up to 100 miles or more on target, using electromagnetic forces. It is a very effective weapon and is employed by Navy battle ships to hit targets at long distances. But if curvature was a reality, the accounting for that curvature would deem this weapon nonfunctional, ineffective, and inoperable. There'd be a 2000 plus meter drop to account for the curve, every time they wish to hit a target from afar.

But the experts argue that the Earth is so big, the curvature is imperceptible. It cannot be readily seen, even at the heights that few aircraft can fly up to. They want us to believe the curvature is there despite what our eyes and other senses tell us. But then how are these same experts going to simultaneously argue that boats, ships, and other things that are far away disappear over the horizon? Either the curvature is detectable or it's not. A side must be picked and stuck to. And not just used out of convenience to justify faulty Science. A side must be picked for congruence to principles. Either curvature is real or it's not. And if it is real, there must be 8 inches of that curvature every mile traveled. It doesn't matter if one is on a highway, a bridge, or in the air, the curvature must be there if we were in fact on a sphere like they keep telling us.

Another way to disprove curvature is using a leveling device the next time you go on a plane. A level is a tool used by carpenters and tradesmen to set nails, lay sheetrock or even hang pictures in straight line. It uses one or more liquid-filled tubes with a bubble and if the bubble is centered between the marked lines, it means the area is level.

Having this level on hand, pay attention to where the bubble is at when the plane is taking off or landing. It is at these times that the level would obviously be off, showing how the tilt of the plane is affecting the instrument. But at cruising altitude, the bubbles on the device remain within the marked areas, showing the plane traveling at level with no tilt whatsoever. But if planes were always have to correct their course to prevent from flying off into outer space, like they should if we were really on a sphere traveling through space at ridiculous speeds, then the leveling device would show it. It would be constantly out of sync and never within the marked lines that show "level-ness" because of the constant course correction that pilots are having to do. But airplanes do exactly what they tell us they do in their name. They fly in the air over a flat plane.

Water is another way to disprove curvature. The surface of water in connected spaces will always settle at the same height, no matter the shape or distance between them. Water in lakes, oceans, or even glass containers will always try to spread out evenly and settle flat. A puddle of water does not begin to curve simply because the puddle gets bigger.

There is no circumstance in which water can curve or bend over a surface. But in the pseudoscience of globe thinking, they want us to believe that water behaves differently than what all the experiments in the history of humanity show. Real Science, however, is observable, measurable, and repeatable. And in every which way, liquids always take the shape of the container they're in, and water will always find its level.

We are told the Earth is spinning at 1,030 mph, which is orbiting the sun at 66,600 mph which is orbiting the center of the galaxy at 514,500 mph which is barreling through space at 1.3 million mph, all the while cosmic wind and space debris are all around. Yet when we look outside, we don't see any of these numbers at play. We don't feel the Earth rotating at over 1,000 mph. This has caused a schism to occur in our psyche where we are no longer able to trust our own senses. Instead, we must trust the information contrary to our experience, so long as it's coming from the experts. But if we really are traveling at those speeds, how is it that the stars are always in the same place in the same seasons?

NASA and modern astronomy say Polaris, the North Star is somewhere between 323-434 light years away or about 1,938,000,000,000 to 2,604,000,000,000,000 miles, making a difference of 666,000,000,000,000 miles. It's not by accident that this set of 6's repeatedly shows up in the math that makes up the astronomy and cosmology of our world.

And how does that same star manage to remain perfectly aligned, straight above the North Pole throughout the Earth's various alleged tilting, wobbling, rotating, and revolving motions.

If the Earth was in fact rotating at the speeds they tell us, then when a helicopter or a drone is to only fly in an upward trajectory and then hover there for a few minutes, it would come back down but land in a different location. That would make the most sense because of the speed that the Earth is supposedly rotating at. But the truth is, it doesn't. These crafts will land in the same exact area they lifted off from.

The same thing happens with a hot air balloon that travels to great heights in the sky but is tethered to the ground. The rotating, tilting, and wobbling at the speeds they claim would create violent and dramatic movements likened to spinning around in circles holding a ballon tethered to a string. When the balloon was to touch back down to the ground, it'd be in a different area than where it took off from. And the people on it would have extreme motion sickness. But this is never seen in real life because those speeds they claim we are traveling at are not happening in real time.

Smoke in the air is something else that puts into question the speeds of the Earth they claim. If there was a big fire somewhere, and a big cloud of smoke can be seen in a distance stemming from that fire, why wouldn't the speed of Earth rotating be more evident in that cloud of smoke.

Or even when an older train that burns coal for fuel and spits out smoke from its exhaust as it travels. Even though these trains move at a much slower speed than that of the Earth spinning, the small cloud of smoke they leave behind in their wake shows the movement of the train. As the engine picks up speed, the smoke stretches out in long, trailing ribbons behind it, whipped by the wind and the motion of the train. And that's because the train is traveling at exponentially slower speeds than they tell us the Earth is.

We are told gravity is the reason we are not able to feel the Earth spinning at over 1,000 mph. And that invisible, magic power called gravity is what keeps the trillions of gallons of ocean water that's on the underside of the Earth from leaking out into outer space. But that same gravity is still weak enough to let an insect or bird fly freely.

And perhaps most curious of all, after centuries of study, gravity is still, technically, just a theory. Not because it's unproven, but because we still don't fully understand why it works the way it does or if it's even the reason why things are the way they are.

The Earth is supposedly tilted on an axis at 23.4 degrees. It just so happens that right angles are 90 degree angles. And if you subtract 23.4 degrees from 90.0 degrees, you are left with 66.6 degrees. The globe-centric cosmological math at it again, rubbing that number in our faces.

NASA is the premiere when it comes to space exploration but when one looks up what NASA actually means in Hebrew, they find that it means "to deceive." Then we take it a step further and look at the logo for NASA and we see there's a serpent's tongue in red, clearly in the background. Genesis 3:13 asks Eve what she has done and she said "The serpent deceived me, and I ate it."

And when we look at who founded NASA, Wernher von Braun, we find that on his gravestone is a quote from Psalms 19.1. It states, "The heavens declare the glory of God and the firmament shows his handywork." It's as if even from his grave, the mocking at our ignorance continues, unencumbered. They know the Earth is flat and that there is a firmament. They just don't want us to know.

All images from NASA are photoshopped or computer-generated images. Any video from the International Space station hovering over the Earth is fake. As you can imagine, 17,500 mph is pretty fast, and at those kinds of speeds, it would be difficult to capture quality images. Plus, all the "space debris" and satellites would make it difficult to maneuver around in an effort to avoid collisions. In fact, any time they show us an image from space, there are never any stars nor satellites in the background. But because we are so fascinated with the actual images that we never pay attention to any of the other details. Details that would debunk that image as fake or photoshopped.

In 1972, the most famous picture of Earth, known as "The Blue Marble" was taken. It appeared in documentaries, album covers, t shirts, stickers, posters, and advertisements. It was claimed to be a picture of the Earth taken from 18,000 miles from the planet's surface. But if you go to Nasa.gov and type in Robert Simmon, AKA Mr. Blue Marble, it will tell you how this CGI photo was really created. They start off by saying they took this photo from low earth orbit. They then went on to say the hard part was creating a flat map of the surface with four months of satellite data. They then wrapped the flat map around a ball and gave us one of the most iconic "photos" ever created.

Two other artists, Robert Hurt and Tim Pyle, are behind some of NASA's most iconic space art in the galaxy. Robert Hurt, an Astrophysicist turned artist and Tim Pyle, once a Hollywood filmmaker, now a planet illustrator, worked together to produce some of NASA's most popular photos and videos. From renderings of how planets light years away could look to actual photos of stars and galaxies captured by NASA telescopes, they take these ideas and grainy pictures and transform them into the art we are shown by the media.

To them, it's all about what the deepest parts of space could look like. They play with color, light, and creativity to create images that are visually astounding and realistic in nature. But realistic does not always equate to real. It's important that we make that distinction.

NASA has a budget of over $22 billion per year. That's more than most Hollywood film studios have and those studios can produce very hyper realistic scenes that show what space can be like. And if they can do that in Hollywood with films, imagine what NASA can do with a much larger budget.

And if they really wanted put the rumors to rest, and dispel any lingering doubts, all that NASA would have to do is show a livestream from space. That livestream could show everyday activities and life happening upside down and sideways on the globe. We'd be shown live video of ships and planes traveling upside down in the underbelly of the globe along with live video feeds showing ships and planes traveling upright on the top side. And the fact that it would all be caught live and in real time would put to rest all doubt about this place we all inhabit.

Encyclopedias before 1958 all describe the shape of the Earth as round, flat, stationary and with upturned edges. They go on to describe a firmament surrounding the Earth as well. All the Encyclopedias after 1958 however no longer describe it that way. That would beg the question, what happened after 1958 that these educational materials no longer described this place the way it used to before?

Neil deGrasse Tyson, one of the more influential proponents of the globe model states that the Earth is actually pear-shaped and has a characteristic wobble to it. That wobble, according to him is evident from "space."

Ironically though, that wobble cannot be seen through high altitude imaging nor felt through any of our senses. But we must trust the expert that it's there, even if all evidence points toward the opposite.

Trusting the experts is what had our parents and grandparents believing that President Nixon received a phone call on a landline, from the astronauts on the moon, 238,000 miles away, and it was all caught on live tv. There are a few problems with that scenario. Number 1, it was a landline in 1969 that the call was made on. Number 2, the fact that the Moon is a luminary, which means it gives off its own light and is not something we can just land on. And number 3, if all of this was in fact true, why have we not been able to return to the moon since then?

They tell us they lost that technology that would allow us to get there. They even go on to say it's not cost-feasible for such a trip, even though their budget is in the billions. And one may even go on to say that a trip to the moon can be a way to dispel any false claims and theories, and to quickly get more people on board with this idea of "space." That, in and of itself would prove its cost feasibility and prove to all the naysayers that we truly do live on a globe.

Timelapse footage of rockets allegedly going into space show a trajectory that is not in line with them actually going into space. The rocket or ship always starts off with shooting straight into the sky, but after a short while, the path of that rocket begins to curve. That curve eventually becomes horizontal to the ground before going out of view. If they really were trying to reach something such as space, they'd fly straight up and keep that trajectory. But then the firmament would become so obvious to the general public that it could not be something they could deny. Especially since there are always so many eyes and media attention to shuttle and rocket launches.

They tell us the reason the trajectories appear as they do has to do with the atmosphere and the shape of the Earth. But our sense of sight cannot be so easily deceived even though our thinking capacity can. If we start paying attention to all the shuttle launches, the truth gets very clear. Especially the way they constantly switch cameras angles at key points to give the illusion of the voyage into space.

According to Science, outer space is a vast vacuum, nearly devoid of matter, where there is no air, no sound can travel, and extreme temperatures reign unchecked by the atmosphere. The flaws with this are too numerous to list but the obvious is that you cannot have air pressure without a container. And you cannot have a vacuum next to air pressure without a barrier in between them.

The firmament is real because we have air pressure here on Earth, therefore there has to be a container. The one example where this law doesn't work is in the Earth's atmosphere, because it demonstrates Earth's air pressure without the presence of a container. This Heliocentric model is the only place where, conveniently, the laws of Science don't apply. But according to them, it's totally normal.

As per more Science, the Earth's crust, which is the outermost layer of the Earth, is supposedly 132,000 feet deep or around 25 miles. The Mantle is the next layer and is 9.5 million feet deep. The Core, which is the center of the Earth is the next layer. These 3 layers interact to shape the Earth's geology, including plate tectonics, volcanic activity, and the magnetic field. So, then the question becomes, how do they even know about the different layers of the Earth, if the deepest hole ever dug is only a little over 40,000 feet deep. That's not even past the first layer but scientists want us to believe they know about all the other layers.

They also want us to believe the center of the Earth is extremely hot, because it's pure lava, which is liquid fire. But then why is the bottom of the ocean extremely cold? In theory, if you are moving closer to the source of the heat, which is the center of the Earth, the deeper you go in the ocean, the hotter the water should become. These are just more examples where the laws of Science conveniently don't apply.

Numerous published papers and studies provide compelling evidence, refuting the conventional narrative as well. These works explore the scientific inconsistencies with the globe model, pointing to an Earth that is fixed and unmoving. For example, a published paper titled "Deviation and Definition of a Linear Aircraft Model" talks about an aircraft of constant mass flying over a flat, nonrotating Earth. Another article written in the Nasa Technical Manual titled "Beacon Position & Altitude Navigation Aided by a Magnetometer," talks about "…flying over a flat non-rotating Earth, and "…with a flat Earth assumption." Another article titled "Propagation of Electromagnetic Fields over a Flat Earth" and "Closed-Form Solution for Ballistic Vehicle Motion" both go onto to state the shape of the Earth in their scientific studies.

Phrases that are constantly used in these studies among so many others are "Earth-fixed coordinate system", "singular arc optimal control", and "Earth-fixed axis system." They all assume the same thing: a flat, non-rotating Earth. All of these studies involve engineering principles that don't account for or compensate for curvature or rotation.

Pilots, ship captains, engineers, and radar technicians all know this fundamental truth. In order for them to get their jobs done effectively and efficiently, they need to understand that the Earth is flat and stationary. By merely doing an online search of these published papers, you can start seeing how the rabbit hole looks and how deep it goes. But mind you that mainstream search engines usually do a good job of filtering information and gatekeeping to keep the shrouds of deception alive and well. They will try to obfuscate and muddy the results so that genuine information stays hidden or at least muddled. The trick is to use a different search engine.

Instruments like the Gyroscope, a Periscope, a compass, a Sundial, an Astrolabe and a Planisphere only work on a flat non-rotating Earth. They could not function if the Earth really was spinning at the speeds they tell us, which are over 1,000 mph. Researchers have also used a camera on a fixed position tripod to record the night sky for months on end. What the recordings show is a night sky that circles around us. It's the stars in the sky that move, not the Earth.

The constellations which are patterns that stars create in the sky are also seen circling us through that fixed point camera system. If we were this space rock spinning and flying through space like they keep telling us, we wouldn't see these same star patterns, nor would the North Star be in the same area, season after season.

Mainstream flat Earth models are often used to distract or discredit deeper cosmological truth. It's a flat Earth psyop released intentionally that mixes incoherent models like a pancake floating in space and tie it to fundamentalist religion to make it seem preposterous and absurd. It's a version designed to mock truth seekers and redirect energy into fruitless debate.

Part of the brainwashing to make us believe that we inhabited this space rock by chance was about getting us to adopt a worldview around a non-Christian foundation. So many movies and cartoons tried to condition us about other galaxies and planets. They wanted us believing that the Earth was a sphere, flying through the vacuum of space. They did it so strategically and so clean that people stopped questioning whether space was real and just assumed that if there's life on this planet, then there must be life on others as well. But God, nor the Bible is nowhere to be found in any of those theories.

History teaches us that the oppressor always trained a few of us to misguide the rest of us. And that's all the globe model and this idea of outer space are designed to do. Misguide and misdirect so we stray away from the truth. The truth that God created this place we inhabit and he carefully constructed the systems in place so that it could be a self-sustaining and self-regenerating system that could stand the test of time. And if He created this place with so much thought and anticipation, imagine what effort He put into creating us.

The truth about where we live, this place we occupy is of paramount importance. Once we realize the magnitude of deception around this place we live, we start seeing all these other lies crumbling before our eyes. Because it's the most fundamental lie and it holds so many other lies in place and together. The deception around where we are, what we're doing here, the Earth beneath our feet, the lights in the sky above us, and even just the true age of this place reveal how Satan has infiltrated education, Science, and even history to kick God out of the picture.

If we've been lied to about all of these, think about what other things begin to get dismantled on their own when the veil gets lifted. Everything from The Big Bang Theory to Evolution crumble under the weight of the Earth's shape and origins. The way life began, the systems in place, how the seasons operate and even our purpose while we're here, all of these are God-ordained.

So, when you look at the potential for a truth like this, a truth that has been suppressed for over 500 years, if it were to get out and it gets revealed that every government, every university, every pundit, and every television station is lying and censoring this truth, trust in these institutions disintegrates almost instantly. The restructuring of society in the system starts in the minds of many and will cause the matrix to begin cracking.

Because more than anything, we find out that we are not as insignificant as we've been led to believe. We find that we were created on purpose, with a purpose, and for a purpose. And we're not just a product of evolution, or coincidence, or chance. We find that even though they tried to hide God from us, Luke 8:17 tells us that "...there is nothing hidden that will not be disclosed, and nothing concealed that will not be made known or brought out into the open." Trust God and study your Bibles. It's all there.

## Chapter 21 – Aliens

*"Aliens are the perfect myth- just enough mystery to believe in, and just enough silences to never prove."* – Author Unknown

A powerful delusion is coming for those who haven't read nor studied their Bible. 2 Thessalonians 2:9-12 talks about how Satan will use all sorts of displays of power through signs and wonders that serve the lie. That lie will revolve around this idea of aliens and UFOs/UAPs. The Bible mentions creatures resembling frogs in Revelation 16:13–14 as part of a vision that John, the author of the book of Revelation had. These "frog-like" beings are symbolic and described as follows: "And I saw three unclean spirits like frogs coming out of the mouth of the dragon, out of the mouth of the beast, and out of the mouth of the false prophet. For they are spirits of demons, performing signs, which go out to the kings of the earth and of the whole world, to gather them to the battle of that great day of God Almighty." (Revelation 16:13–14, NKJV)

These creatures are what everyone, including the media will refer to as aliens when the great reveal happens. During this time, a great deception will ensue. Even though frogs are amphibians, they do closely resemble what we know to be reptiles and that's what many believe these demons look like in their physical form. And many believe that's why they put out movies and shows that portray aliens in the way they do. They have been priming us for this eventual reveal. Pre-programming or pre-conditioning us so that when it does finally happen, people will be convinced it's these extra-terrestrial beings from another planet. And that will be their confirmation that they knew all along that they weren't alone in the universe. Area 51, unexplained phenomena in the skies, and even movies based off of "true events" have been training the masses to easily accept these "truths" when they are formally made public.

But these "aliens" are not from another planet. They are part of the 1/3 of the angels that became demons when they followed Satan and defied God. They've been at work, moving amongst the shadows at the behest of Satan since their fall from Heaven. And because they have been here for so long, they have great knowledge and an even greater understanding of human behavior, psychology, physics and engineering. Their technology will be way more advanced than what we can imagine and it may even look like magic. They will have aircraft that seems to defy physics, and will resemble what we've been taught UFOs and UAPs look like. And because they are known to be interdimensional beings, they will seem to appear and disappear at a whim. But we should not be deceived, for these are just parlor tricks and do not compare to the real power of the one true God.

Their goal is and always has been to defile mankind and in turn try to hurt God. They will do this through deception, control, and separation from truth. Satan and his demons live under this way of doing things so that if they tell you in advance what's to occur, then they feel they are free from the spiritual consequences. In this way, they feel like there is no karmic retribution on their end, because they told us what was to happen in advance. They tell us through movies, shows, and cartoons. They show us what aliens could look like and the technology they are capable of producing. And they even foreshadow and foretell events way in advance before the idea of those things happening is even a possibility. That goes to show the strategy in play that Satan and these demonic entities are employing. It's a long game that's been in process for some time. But we are nearing the final quarter, so the tactics have been ramping up, and their brazenness has been increasing dramatically.

As of now, these demons have been working in the shadows, but they will make their appearance formal and widely known around the time of the Rapture or close to the end of days. Some believe they will try and convince the masses that they are the ones who took all the people who were raptured. Hysteria will flood the streets, delirium and frenzy will inundate social media, and non-believers and believers alike will question everything. That's the point. Their goal is to create confusion and doubt. Doubt in God, uncertainty in purpose, confusion about everything they've been taught.

At this point, someone will be introduced that supposedly will be able to help the rest of the people who were left behind. This entity will be the Antichrist in human form, and for three and a half years, his policies do appear to be positive, hopeful, and supportive of all. There will be peace and prosperity like never before. However, the second part of his reign, the second three and a half years will be a much different story.

During this time a one world religion will be adopted, as well as a one world currency. The mark of the beast will be employed, though under a different name. The idea is that only those that have it will be allowed to buy or sell anything. Food, groceries, gas, water, all will be subject to this novel payment system. Anyone refusing the mark will be made an example of. It will be during this time that the persecution against Christians that were left behind will be the hardest and most difficult. And anyone who does accept the mark will forfeit their place in heaven and be condemned to eternal separation from God and eternal punishment along Satan.

This 7 year reign by the Antichrist will culminate with a great war where Heavenly angels battle against Satan and his demons. The Bible does prophesy all this and one can get a better picture of what this entails by reading the Books of Daniel, Ezekiel, Isaiah, Zechariah, Thessalonians and Revelation. But the main takeaway is that Satan will try to use "Aliens" as a way to explain the Rapture, and to disprove the existence of God.

If they can get us to doubt the existence of God, which is why this "rotating globe Earth floating in space" idea is pushed so heavily, then they can get us to pretty much do anything, even if it goes against biblical principles. But for those who have kept up with their Bible, they won't be caught off guard. Because they know how the story begins and how it ends.

The use of lasers and hologram projections will be another way that mass panic, confusion, and the questioning of beliefs will come into play. In its early stages, these lasers and hologram projections are being used to simulate scenarios, such as a whale floating in the sky as if it was swimming in the ocean or a huge phoenix flying around the audience. These technologies are already being used in professional sports and music arenas and even Times Square in NYC. Companies are now using this technology to advertise the same way billboards used to. But the sophistication of these technologies has been increasing exponentially and now even drones are being added to the mix to bring about a more life-like and realistic experience.

With this technology, a false alien invasion, a messianic return, or some kind of world-changing phenomena can be simulated and made to look like it's happening in real time. This fake global event can be used to unify the world under a single authoritarian regime, making it easier to bring about Bible prophecy without calling it Bible prophecy.

In such a scenario, mass fear and confusion could be created through a coordinated display of holographic projections, visible worldwide that looks hyper-realistic. A giant celestial phenomena, false religious icons, or "other-worldly" spacecraft could be used to convince people that a supernatural or extraterrestrial event is unfolding. Combined with manipulated news, emergency broadcasts, and psychological operations, people could be driven into confusion, fear, and submission, potentially accepting global control out of desperation for safety and order. With this in play, the Antichrist, the mark of the beast, and any other outrageous requirement will be more easily accepted by the majority. At this point, prophecy will be well underway, and Armageddon is soon to follow.

This idea about aliens and creatures from another planet goes hand in hand with the globe model and eliminates God from the equation. Over the years, we have been subtly and persistently conditioned to believe in the existence of aliens through a steady stream of kids' cartoons, sci-fi movies, novels, and mass media.

From playful green Martians in Saturday morning shows to dramatic extraterrestrial encounters in blockbuster films, these portrayals have woven the idea of alien life into our cultural imagination. Even books and news reports have blurred the line between fiction and possibility, reinforcing the narrative that alien life is not only real but imminent. As a result, belief in extraterrestrials has shifted from fringe speculation to a mainstream curiosity.

But as James 1:16 states, "Do not be fooled, my beloved brothers and sisters." Discernment and trust in God will be paramount in these coming times. Because there is no such thing as aliens and there aren't other planets beyond our galaxy from which they came. They are fallen angels which we know as demons. And their enmity towards God will have them on a mission to hurt Him and his people in any and every which way they can. In the face of this growing deception and spiritual confusion, we are called to stand firm in our faith, grounded in truth and unwavering in conviction.

The enemy may disguise himself through signs, wonders, and even the illusion of alien life, but we are not without guidance or defense. By clinging to God's Word and walking in the light of Christ, we can resist the guile of these demonic forces and endure the trials to come with courage and clarity. Now more than ever, our strength must be rooted in faith, not fear

# Conclusion

*"I have fought the good fight, I have finished the race, I have kept the faith."* - Timothy 4:7

The number of fallen angels that came down with Satan has not changed nor multiplied. It's still the same number as in the initial fall. Because of this, Satan has to be very cunning and astute as to create a system by which he could multiply darkness and make it seem like he is omnipotent. So, he doesn't have to attack every generation. He just needs to program the first generation to believe certain things and then those beliefs get passed down.

These limiting beliefs are designed to drown out the promises that the word of God tells us. So, when one generation agrees with a captivity mindset, they teach the next generation, and by the third and fourth generation, nobody bothers to question it because it's now culture and has become the new normal. That's how Satan maintains the status quo.

There's a battle of potential happening against our children. When Satan was cast out of Heaven along with a third of the angels, he knew that his decision would have eternal effects and consequences. There would be no going back. The redemption of the blood of Jesus Christ does not cover him and he will never be allowed to return. Because of that, there is a hatred which we cannot fathom from Satan for our children. Even if they stumble, even if they fall, even if they depart like the prodigal son, when they do decide to return to the Lord, there'll be a robe and a ring ready and waiting for them. Your child will be adopted into the Kingdom of Heaven and Satan can never have that. Christ did not die for Satan and Christ's blood does not cover him nor his followers.

And so there is this intense hatred for the offspring and an immense enmity towards God. Hatred that our sons and daughters could choose Jesus and be adopted back to the table which Lucifer once sat at. That is why Satan has been attacking us through our children and through agendas that target them for quite some time. Whether it be a vaccine schedule designed to contaminate the temple that is our bodies, an agenda designed around removing God and biblical principles from the equation, or the control of information, painting lies as truth and truth as lies, Satan has been on the attack, relentless and ruthless.

Now more than ever, it's important to "Submit yourselves therefore to God, resist the devil and he will flee from you." This means you cannot resist the devil if you don't submit yourself to God. Romans 12:1 says, "I beseech you therefore, by the mercies of God, to present your bodies as a living sacrifice." Our bodies want to control us and at the same time kill us. Our flesh is suicidal in that regard because it loves to do the things that are not good for us and it hates to do the things that are good for us.

The nature of our flesh is sinful, slothful, and gluttonous. That's why we have to bring it under subjugation. We must see it like this: because the sovereignty of God is supreme, we must present our bodies a living sacrifice. This can be likened to what is known as a continual burnt offering, because a burnt offering is a picture of a total sacrifice. The burnt offering means it's all consumed for

God. There's nothing leftover, so I get nothing. That's the picture of the burnt offering. The word sacrifice means to let go of something of a lower nature so you can take a hold of something of a higher nature.

Good is the greatest enemy to great and it's why so many stay stuck in the good, the okay, the "not that bad." But we owe it to our Creator, our God, our Lord that we strive for the great. Because it's never about the goals we achieve, but it's always about the person we become in pursuit of those goals. There is power in the pursuit.

New Age philosophies teach about living a spiritual life and have blended a cornucopia of religions into an old idea about love, light, energy, and chakras. And even though there are bits of truth spread throughout, where is God and where is Jesus in it? It's not so much about seeking the spiritual life but rather living a spirit-filled life. A life filled with the Holy Spirit and guided by biblical principles.

There's a lot of confusion right now and it's driving general, vague spirituality, deconstructionism, progressive Christianity, Wokism, BLM Christians, and the Rainbow flag pastors to seem to be what Christianity is supposed to look like. But all we need to do is get back to the Bible and the standards set forth in there. Jesus loved the sinner but hated the sin. Whenever Jesus healed someone, he always told them after to "go and sin no more." We cannot continue living in sin, unrepented and profess to be saved. And justify it by saying God loves us all just the way we are.

The principles laid out in the Bible are straight forward and congruent. They're not the cherry-picked pieces that align with a narrative or an agenda for society. And globalism is not a goal that Christians should seek. Because in a globalized system, pressure often mounts for all religions to be treated as equal paths or blended into a universal belief system.

And the Bible tells us Jesus is the way, the truth, and the life. No one goes to God except through Him. Globalism pushes toward "tolerance" and that actually morphs into intolerance of this biblical exclusivity. And in the end, it will set the stage for the "one-world government" and one-world religion warned about in Revelation. In essence, all roads lead to prophecy and prophecy is laid out in the Bible.

It's important to note that the very people that push for Atheism do believe in God. They're throwing rituals either in private or center stage to counter God and it's all to bring the devil forward. And because they are pop culture celebrities and athletes, they can do it in a way where it seems like harmless trendsetting. But they know God exists, they just don't want everyone else to know. Because if that truth became so overwhelmingly evident, everyone would start thinking and acting from a biblical standpoint. The sin that was once glorified would cease almost immediately. And Satan would lose his footing indefinitely. Isaiah 45:23, Romans 14:11, and Philippians 2:10-11 all mention how every knee shall bow and every tongue will confess to God. So, it's only a matter of time before the world truly finds out who the real, one true God really is.

Satan's tactics are simple. He will make sin look normal and righteousness look weird. God is calling us to not be driven by emotion but rather to be driven by discipline. To be driven by choice. It's harder, but it's also better. It's about learning to walk by faith and disregarding the carnal inclinations.

The devil is going to be coming into our lives and accusing us with all sorts of lies. He'll be telling us we are not who we once were, or how we are shadows of our previous selves or even how our past will stop us from being good with God. All of these are lies that Satan will use to diminish our capacity for better. We must remember that we are covered by the same blood that made us righteous, the same blood that saved us, the same blood that was sacrificed for our sin. What Jesus did for us on the cross cannot be diminished by Satan's lies and deceptions.

The devil doesn't come to us with a red face, pointy tail, horns and a trident. He comes to us disguised as everything we've always wanted. Satan and his demons analyze us and have been for quite some time. They act as monitoring spirits, analyzing our weaknesses and strengths. They listen to our conversations and to when we said something out of frustration, weakness, or despair. They will then act on that information and will keep prying on that one weakness over and over.

We have to become conscious of how they are prying on that weakness. And then we have to praise God, because demons hate it when we praise God. When we praise God, it releases a heavenly fragrance, an aroma that drives demons away. King David in the Book of Psalm talked about how his praise was like a fragrance unto the Lord (Psalm 141:2). The fragrance of praise makes demons terrified and curl, they hate it. Many people who are dealing with spiritual onslaught and attacks, the question becomes, have you praised God at all during those times?

We don't worship and praise just to make it go away. We should do it so consistent, that it becomes our lifestyle. And in that, demons cannot pry for long on those weaknesses that we confessed in a moment. Because worship is our weapon and demons hate praise more than they enjoy the satisfaction of attacking.

We are living in a time when at first, evil is simply overlooked and eventually permitted. Later, it is legalized and so many are there to promote it. Then it is celebrated and anyone who still calls it evil is persecuted. But Isaiah 5:20 states "Woe unto them who call evil good, and good evil." It is imperative to draw discernment from the Holy Spirit daily because Satan's pawns have been hard at work changing labels and distorting truths.

They want us to believe abortion and the murder of babies is a woman's right to choose because it's "her body, her choice." Homosexuality, which is an abomination according to scripture is now labeled as pride and protested with a rainbow flag. Addictions are labeled as diseases with genetic predispositions. Fornication is just casual sex, idolatry is just veneration, and lust is just admiration.

But we have to start seeing things as they are and not how we'd like them to be. Because society can easily have us thinking what is wrong is right and what is right is wrong.

It can have us rationalizing bad behaviors and poor actions. But we were not called to trivialize sin. We were called to repent of it and "sin no more" as Jesus told so many that he healed.

Jesus didn't just eat with sinners and tax collectors because He wanted to appear inclusive, tolerant or accepting. He ate with them to call them to a changed and fruitful life. To die to self and live for Him. His call is a transformation of life, not an affirmation of identity. We must start disciplining ourselves to do what we need to do, regardless if we feel like doing it or not.

Discipline is the strongest form of self love. It's ignoring something you want right now for something better later on. Discipline reveals the commitment you have to yourself, your family, and all the generations to follow. Especially on days you don't want to. Your future you is depending on the current you to keep the promises you made to yourself yesterday.

Life gets harder than it needs to be when all you do is what is easy. But on the flip side, life gets easier when you do what is hard. Making time for God is hard. Creating routines where you pray and give thanks is hard. Exercising for you body, mind, and spirit are hard. Putting God first in everything is hard. But in doing these hard things, life starts to flow more smoothly and in turn, life does get easy. Do the hard things.

Imagine how valuable your soul must be for Satan to tirelessly pursue it and for the King of Kings to lay down his own life for it. But drifting away from God is not so hard. It's a slow fade that rarely gets noticed until the distance between has grown so much. Think of it this way. Imagine that you and a friend are at a concert. Your friend is trying to talk to you, but because he is whispering, you can hardly hear what he is saying. If you weren't at a concert but rather a quiet place, it'd be easier to hear them. But because you are in a noisy, crowded place, you try to focus on his lips to read what he's saying. But because distractions are everywhere, it's so easy to get lost in the moments.

So, after a while, you stop looking to your friend because you're so engrossed in what you're doing that by the time you remember your friend, he's nowhere to be found. You don't know where he went, how long he'll be, or even if he'll be back. All you know is you lost yourself in a moment, absorbed and spellbound. So much so that the only person you really knew and who knew you is no longer by your side, nor anywhere to be found. In this, it's not so hard to feel alone, even if surrounded by a crowd.

This is similar to our walk with God. The world can sometimes be very loud, with distractions, diversions, interruptions, and interference everywhere. Knowing this, the goal is to always be in close proximity with God. Because the closer we are to Him, the easier it is hear His Voice, even if it's just a whisper.

And if we cannot hear his voice, so long as we are close by and looking to Him, we could at least read his lips or get a better idea of what he's trying to tell us. It's so easy to drift off course and become disconnected, just going through the motions. That's why intention and proximity matter. And in life, if we feel like this has already happened, we must confess our sins immediately and wholeheartedly seek Him. John 1:19 tells us "If we confess our sins, he is faithful and just and will forgive us our sins and purify us from all unrighteousness." But then we must consciously choose to stay connected so that we don't drift away again.

When light confronts darkness, there can be an uncomfortableness. Because it will shine a light and bring into focus all those things we have grown to see as normal or at least acceptable. But scripture reminds us that we cannot love the things of this world and love Jesus simultaneously. We cannot love sin and love God at the same time. Ephesians 5:11 tells us "Have no fellowship with the fruitless deeds of darkness but rather expose them." Sometimes we have to expose them to ourselves through reflection and other times we have to expose them to others. But it's not from a soapbox infused with judgement. It's from a place of love and understanding but also from a place of warning. Because when the end comes, we cannot say we didn't know, or they never told us.

Light does nullify darkness but we must shine it on purpose, and we have to act on what gets revealed. Because Ephesians 13-14 says "... all things become visible when exposed to light. For this reason, it says "Awake sleeper and arise from the dead." How many have been in this slumber, sleepwalking through life? We can only push things so far down the road, avoiding and neglecting to deal with what will eventually and ultimately need to be dealt with.

It's been said that the Earth and the Heavens have the same birthdate and so it is impossible to function on the

Earth without consulting with the Heavens. That's why it's important to "Seek ye first the kingdom of God and all other things will be given unto thee" as Matthew 6:33 says. So along with praying, giving thanks, and talking to God, focus on putting him at the center of everything. It's not just about saying that Jesus is Lord and then living according to worldly standards. It's about living this truth with whole-hearted belief. And even though this is probably the most powerful strategy, it is easily the hardest one to abide by.

Because putting God first above all things is about trusting that no matter how things look, they will turn out exactly the way they're supposed to. It's also about putting our wants and desires to the side and living for Him first. It's about crucifying the flesh to break free from the carnality that is what we believe to be us.

If we say we love our partner but we're cheating on them behind their back, do we truly love them? Many profess they love Jesus but then are doing the very things that He died on the cross to set us free from. So even though we may say we love Him, our actions are revealing otherwise. Jesus said those who love me obey my commands.

So, if we truly love him, then we're going to have to submit to him, and trust in his direction. We do this because we know God's will is good. God's plans for our life are good. That's why he gives commands, because he sees the bigger picture. Our job is to put God first and trust the process that comes with that.

So how does one spell Love? The obvious answer is L-O-V-E but the truer answer is really T-I-M-E. Time is how love is really shown and demonstrated. We make time for the things we value and if we value something, that's our way of showing it some love. If we find that we just don't have time to do certain things, it's because we haven't got to the point that we value them at the level we should. Look at it this way. The more you hang out with certain friends, the bigger the connection you create, the stronger the bond you develop. That's how it is with anything, be it people, material items, games, the world and even God the Father.

Strengthen your connection with God by constantly talking with him and staying in close communion with him. The more time we spend with the Lord, reading his word, in prayer, and living in congruence with biblical principles, the stronger we get. Ephesians 6 tells us that the word of God is our sword of the Spirit. It is our primary weapon and should be sharpened and exercised often. This is so that when it's really needed, we'd know how to use it, and use it well.

When we first begin our Christian walk, we may feel unstoppable, strong, ready, and sure of ourselves. We believe we can stand our ground, no matter what comes, and take on any challenge head-on. But God calls us to something greater. He wants us to love one another deeply, to lift each other up, to offer a hand when the load is heavy, and to keep each other anchored in truth. Because the longer we try to go it alone, the heavier the journey becomes.

 Some will still choose to push ahead by themselves for as long as they can, and that's okay. But eventually, the moment comes when the truth sinks in: we were never meant to walk this road alone. Together, we can go farther, faster. God gives us strength when we stand together, but there will also be moments when we must stand alone. In those times, it should never be out of pride or stubbornness, but out of the quiet confidence that God is with us, even when we can't feel Him. That's the very place where faith is put into action. And whatever is exercised, is strengthened.

Life sometimes makes more sense in reverse. It's not easy to connect the dots as we live through something we don't understand. But in looking back, we can always see why things turned out the way they did. We can more clearly see why things had to happen the way they happened.

It's like they say, hindsight is always 20/20. And so by being grateful and giving thanks in advance, we are helping to create that clarity early on. We are preparing our headspace so that even though we may not know why things are happening the way they are, they're happening for a greater good that will get clearer as we go. We take on that optimism and in doing so, reduce our need to fret over the challenges that were meant to make us better.

Afterall, that's what challenges do, or at least that's what they're supposed to do. The purpose of any challenge is to induce growth and force us to rise to the occasion. To push us beyond our comfort, so that we can stretch and grow. Just like with muscles, our mindset, perspective and perception all expand by demand. The more they are trained, the better they get. The better they get, the better we become. The better we become, the better our life gets. So even though we may have "unanswered" prayers and we struggle to see what God's doing good in our life, we must remember that there are always blessings to be thankful for. It's just that sometimes we have to stop and think on purpose. Because appreciation doesn't always happen on its own. Especially when we are so hypnotized by the world and all these worldly things that we rarely take time to deliberately stop and think on purpose. We are so easily and willfully distracted that we can't find the time to spend in communion with God.

But this is a long game and so we must fix our eyes on the prize. Our existence here on Earth is merely a parenthesis in eternity. We must stop living as if consequences from the way we live here won't have an effect on the way we live in the after. Life really is short but eternity happens to be very long. For many, it's hard to grasp what that truly means. We are here for a short time in this thing we call life, but because our soul is infinite, it will live on long after the body dies. That begs the question, what happens after?

A simple fact that many "powers that be" want you to doubt is that Heaven is for real. And if that's really the case, then so is Hell. The way we live our lives here, the way we go about our journey in this place determines where we go after. I know there are a lot of shows that want us to believe that there's this middle ground where we can stay when we die, or that we may get another chance through a new body when we pass. That is beyond my scope of knowing, but what I do know is, the way we go about our lives here determines so much in the after.

2 Corinthians 5:10 says "For we must all appear before the judgment seat of Christ, so that each of us may receive

what is due us for the things done while in the body, whether good or bad." Revelation 20:12 states "And I saw the dead, great and small, standing before the throne, and books were opened. Another book was opened, which is the book of life. The dead were judged according to what they had done as recorded in the books." So, what we do and how we do it matters greatly.

It's easy to grow weary and tired from denying yourself the things that the flesh may want or that the world has conditioned you to think you need. It's easy to get complacent and do just enough to get by. But we need to stand up and fight. Fight to ensure our families have a fighting chance. Stand up and fight to ensure the ones that come after will have better opportunities. Stand up and fight the attacks of the enemy who seeks to destroy all that is good and all that is of God. We cannot take this lightly because there is so much at stake. Jesus Christ died on the cross for our sins and so the price has been paid.

But we need to recognize there are deceptions all around and the enemy wants us to feel engulfed and overwhelmed by them. But Romans 12:2 reminds us "…not to conform to the pattern of this world but be transformed by the renewing of our mind. Then we will be able to test and approve what God's will is."

Scripture does say there are two destinations, Heaven or Hell. It talks of two ways, the narrow or the broad. It states there are two masters, Christ or Satan. And there are two walks, the spirit or the flesh. Even though so many are half-way believers, there's no halfway point in any of these. To believe something, we must wholeheartedly accept it with absolute certainty. There is no room for doubt or unbelief. There is only conviction of what is true and nothing else can impede it from being true.

So, if Satan cannot blind the people that believe, then he will try to divide them. He will try to destroy their influence for God. In the court of public opinion, one can easily be made to look like they're crazy or off their meds or just a conspiracy theorist. These labels tend to diminish the influence rather quickly, even if all that was being said or written was truthful. Many ideas and facts are quickly dismissed if they are not aligned with a narrative that has been asserted for so long. Important truths tend to get tossed by the wayside and the worldly deception from Satan continues, unencumbered.

But in this age of information, now's the time to awaken to truth. Satan is the enemy, and his ultimate plan is to hurt God in any and every way he can. Deception, disinformation, and defamation are just a few of the ways he will go about it.

Though Satan is powerful, his power is limited by God. He can only act with God's permission as Job 1:12 and Job 2:6 tells us. He is ultimately subject to God's authority. If we are truly Christians and have the Holy Spirit living within us, Satan cannot defeat us. He will try to make it seem like he can. He will tempt the flesh and try to drive us into sin. He will flood the mind with thoughts and anxiety and cause us to doubt the goodness of God. He will even play tricks on us, making it seem like he's more powerful than he really is.

But if we are going about our daily lives walking in the spirit, meaning, staying in close contact with God through prayer, presence in state of mind, and the denying of the flesh, we don't need to be walking around afraid. We should respect Satan and his demons to a certain extent, but in no way cower before them. They are not equal nor even remotely close to be in the same vicinity as the Most High. And God has given us everything we need to be victorious against everything Satan brings to the table.

But we cannot be casual about it. Because if we are favored by God, then we are also to be favored by Satan. His goal is to destroy our capacity to do what God has called us to do. So, with great favor comes great responsibility.

A conversation we were meant to have with God that we didn't, Satan will have it with us. But we must give him no ground and stand firm in our convictions. Because he is after our confidence, our peace, our joy, our heart, our mind, our soul, our purpose, and our fruit. 1 Peter 5:8 tells us "Be sober and be vigilant because your adversary the devil, as a roaring lion, walks about seeking whom he can devour."

Have those conversations with God, go to Him for everything. Don't just ignore the thoughts, temptations, or anxiety. Put it all at his feet because He wants us to rely on Him. We weren't designed to do this all on our own. Just like a battery powered tool. It does have power on its own and can function for a limited time on that power. But when it's connected to an outlet, a power source, it has way more power and for longer. The same applies to us. But our power source is God, and we stay connected by abiding in His word and living according to scripture.

Satan knows our name but calls us by our failures. But Jesus knows our failures and calls us by our name. As followers of Christ, we are called to live lives rooted in the word of God, reflecting the love, the grace, and the truth of Jesus in all we do. Scripture reminds us that our obedience today helps to lay the foundation for the blessings tomorrow. And not only for ourselves but for the generations to follow. When we walk in righteousness, preach the Gospel boldly, and help bring others to Christ, we become vessels of God's eternal purpose.

Our faithfulness can open doors for our children and our children's children to inherit the kingdom of heaven. This creates a legacy of spiritual strength and divine favor. Because of this, we must live intentionally, guided by God's truth, so that through our witness, many may come to know Jesus. And in doing that, we help pull the curtain back and expose the real enemy everyone is overlooking.

## Prayer to Invite Jesus Christ Into Your Life and Renew Your Relationship with God

Heavenly Father, I come before You today with a humble heart, acknowledging that I am in need of Your grace and mercy. I confess my sins and ask for Your forgiveness. I believe that Jesus Christ is Your son, that he died on the cross for my sins and that He rose again so I could have eternal life. Lord Jesus, I invite You into my heart, Be my Savior, my Lord, my King.

I surrender my old ways and ask to be born again through the power of the Holy Spirit. Wash me clean, renew my mind, and transform my heart. Fill me with Your spirit so I may walk in truth, live in righteousness, and follow You all the days of my life.

Today I choose to walk in a new direction, with You Father God. Lead me, guide me, and use me to fulfill your purpose. Strengthen my faith, surround me with Your peace, and help me to grow in Your word daily. Thank you for saving me, for making me new, and for giving me the promise of eternal life. In Jesus' name I pray, Amen.

# Bibliography

Al Ozonoff, Etsuro Nanishi, Ofer Levy. *"Bell's Palsy and SARS-Cov-2 Vaccines".* The Lancet. www.thelancet.com/journals/laninf/article/PIIS1473

Andrea Michelson. *"Chemicals in shampoo and makeup are linked to early death, study finds".* 2021

Aaron Siri. www.Aaronsiri.substack.com

Baletti, Brenda Ph.D. *"Government Misled Public on Thimerosal Link To Autism "for Decades*," Falsely Claims It's Been Removed From Vaccines." Childrenshealthdefense.org. April 2025.

Bornali Bhattacharjee, Peiwen Lu, Valter Silva Monteiro, Alexandra Tabachnikova, Kexin Wang, William B. Hooper, Victoria Bastos, Kerrie Greene, Mitsuaki Sawano, Christian Guirgis, Tiffany J. Tzeng, Frederick Warner Pavlina Baevova, Kathy Kamath, Jack Reifert, Danice Hertz, Brianne Dressen, Laura Tabacof, Jamie Wood, Lily Cooke, Mackenzie Doerstling, Shadan Nolasco, Amer Ahmed, Amy Proal, David Putrino, Leying Guan, Harlan M. Krumholz, Akiko Iwasaki . "Antigenic Signatures Associated with Chronic Illnesses after 1 COVID-19 Vaccination". Med RXIV. *Immunological and Antigenic Signatures Associated with Chronic Illnesses after COVID-19 Vaccination.*2025

Braude, Gerald, Informed Choice Washington.*www.informedchoicewa.substack.com*.2025

*"Chemtrails: The exotic Weapon"*. Usafa. Alachuacounty.us.2014

David Nield. *"Most COVID-19 Deaths May Be The Result of A Completely Different Infection"*. Science Alert. 2023. Most COVID-19 Deaths May Be The Result of a Completely Different Infection : ScienceAlert

Dr. Bryan Ardis. *"Moving Beyond The COVID-19 Lies"*.2024

Dr. William H. Gaunt,NMD & Spencer M. Gaunt RN. *"Unvaccinated Children Are Healthier Than Vaccinated Counterparts"*. www.jenifermargulis.net

Dr. Vladamir Zelenko. www.Vladimirzelenkomd.com

Gao, Catherine A., et al. "Machine Learning Links Unresolving Secondary Pneumonia to Mortality in Patients with Severe Pneumonia, Including COVID-19." *Journal of Clinical Investigation*, vol. 132, no. 5, 2022, pp. e170682. DOI:10.1172/JCI170682.

Guthrie, Matthew. *www.followthesilenced.com*. 2025

Hulscher, Nicolas. *"Autopsy findings in cases of fatal Covid-19 vaccine-induced myocarditis"*. PubMed. 2024

Harlan M Krumholz , Yilun Wu , Mitsuaki Sawano , Rishi Shah , Tianna Zhou , Adith S Arun , Pavan Khosla , Shayaan Kaleem, Anushree Vashist , Bornali

Bhattacharjee , Qinglan Ding , Yuan Lu , César Caraballo , Frederick Warner , Chenxi Huang , Jeph Herrin, David Putrino , Danice Hertz , Brianne Dressen , Akiko Iwasaki. *"Post-Vaccination Syndrome: A Descriptive Analysis of Reported Symptoms and Patient Experiences After Covid-19 Immunization".* 2023 Nov 10:2023.11.09.23298266. [Version 1] doi: 10.1101/2023.11.09.23298266

Judy George. *"Researchers Describe Rare Syndrome After COVID Vaccine".* MedPage Today. February 20, 2025

Krawczyk, P.S., Mazur, M., Orzeł, W. et al. *"Re-adenylation by TENT5A enhances efficacy of SARS-CoV-2 mRNA vaccines".* Nature (2025). https://doi.org/10.1038/s41586-025-08842-1

*"Lasting immunity found after recovery from COVID-19".* National Institute of Health. 2021

Nicolas Hulscher, Roger Hodkinson, William Makis, Peter A McCullough. *"Autopsy findings in cases of fatal COVID-19 vaccine-induced myocarditis.* PMID 38221509. 2024

Mallory Locklear." *Immune Markers of Post-Vaccination Syndrome Indicate Future Research Directions."* Feb 19, 2025

Maria Tsikala Vafea , Raina Zhang , Markos Kalligeros , Evangelia K Mylona , Fadi Shehadeh , Eleftherios Mylonakis. "Mortality in mechanically ventilated patients with COVID-19: a systematic review". 2021 May. 18 (5):457-471. doi: 10.1080/17434440.2021.1915764. Epub 2021 Apr 30.

McCullough, P. A. (2023). *"SV40 promoters and enhancers contaminate Pfizer-BioNTech COVID-19 vaccine".* Courageous Discourse.

McKernan, K., Helbert, Y., Kane, L. T., & McLaughlin, S. (2023). *"Sequencing of bivalent Moderna and Pfizer mRNA vaccines reveals nanogram to microgram quantities of expression vector dsDNA per dose".* https://doi.org/10.31219/osf.io/b9t7m

Miller, Neil Z. "Vaccines and Sudden Infant Death: An Analysis of the VAERS Database 1990–2019 and Review of the Medical Literature." *Toxicology Reports*, vol. 8, 24 June 2021, pp. 1324–1335. Elsevier, doi:10.1016/j.toxrep.2021.06.020.

Nicolas Hulscher et al. ESC Heart Fail. *"Autopsy findings in cases of fatal COVID-19 vaccine-induced myocarditis."* PubMed.2024.

Nicola Jones. *"Does using ChatGPT change your brain activity? Study sparks debate."* www.nature.com/articles/d41586-02005-y. 2025.

Paul Thomas MD. Paulthomasmd.com

Prof. Dr. Arne Burkhardt, Prof. Dr. Walter Lang. *"New Histopathological Insights Into Covid vaccine injuries".* March 12, 2022.

Rogers, Toby MD. *"Mapping the Entire Field of Autism."* (2025). https://tobyrogers.substack.com/p/mapping-the-entire-field-of-autism

Rogers, Toby MD. *"The True Cost of Autism"*. Children's Health Defense Fund. 2020

Swiss Policy Research. *"A Systematic Overview of Severe Covid Adverse Events."* April 2023.

Schnoebelen, William. *"Masonry: Beyond The Light"*. March 1, 1991

Saplakoglu, Yasemin. *"Nearly 9 in 10 Patients Who Are Put On A Ventilator Die, New York Hospital Data Suggests"*. April 23. 2020

Shah, K. V., & Nathanson, N. (1976). *"Human exposure to SV40: Review and comment"*. American Journal of Epidemiology, 103(1), 1–12.
Substack (https://anandamide.substack.com/p/why-is-a-fauci-hiv-vax-sequence-in?utm_source=substack&publication_id=456768&post_id=162261550&utm_medium=email&utm_content=share&utm_campaign=email-share&triggerShare=true&isFreemail=false&r=jhcie&triedRedirect=true)

Shrestha, Nabin K., et al. *Effectiveness of the 2024–2025 Influenza Vaccine in Preventing Infection in Healthcare Personnel*. medRxiv, 27 Mar. 2025, doi:10.1101/2025.03.26.25324567. Preprint.

Simonsen, Lone, et al. "Impact of Influenza Vaccination on Seasonal Mortality in the US Elderly Population." *Archives of Internal Medicine*, vol. 165, no. 3, 14 Feb.

2005, pp. 265–272. American Medical Association, doi:10.1001/archinte.165.3.265.

Sivan Gazit, MD MA; Roei Shlezinger, BA; Galit Perez MN MA; Roni Lotan, PhD. *"Comparing SARS CoV-2 natural immunity to vaccine-induced immunity; reinfection versus breakthrough infections"*. Med RXIV 2021.

Testimony on Vaccines and Neurodevelopmental Disorders. Neuenschwander, James. "Testimony on Vaccines and Neurodevelopmental Disorders." *U.S. Court of Federal Claims*, www.govinfo.gov/content/pkg/USCOURTS-cofc-1_17-vv-00109/pdf/USCOURTS-cofc-1_17-vv-00109-0.pdf?utm_source

TGE Media. *Frankenskies Documentary*. www.thegloablelite.org

"The Age of Autism: Mercury, Medicine, and a Man-Made Epidemic" Olmsted, Dan, and Mark Blaxill. *The Age of Autism: Mercury, Medicine, and a Man-Made Epidemic*. Thomas Dunne Books, 2010.

"The Amish Anomaly" Olmsted, Dan. "The Amish Anomaly." *United Press International*, 19 Apr. 2005, www.upi.com/Science_News/2005/04/19/The-Age-of-Autism-The-Amish-anomaly/95661113911795/.

"The Amish Elephant" Olmsted, Dan. "The Amish Elephant." *United Press International*, 29 Oct. 2005, www.upi.com/Health_News/2005/10/29/The-Age-of-Autism-The-Amish-Elephant/44901130610898/.

"The Gut, GI, and Autism" Neuenschwander, James. "The Gut, GI, and Autism." *NeuroNeeds*,
www.neuroneeds.com/the-gut-gi-and-autism/?utm

"Research on Gut Issues, Immune System Dysfunction, and Autism". Neuenschwander, James. "Gut Issues, Immune System Dysfunction, and Brain Inflammation in Autism." *Bio Energy Medical Center*, www.bioenergymedicalcenter.com/blog/gut-issues-immune-system-dysfunction-brain-inflammation-in-autism?utm

The Corvelva Team. *"New Data Shows DNA From Aborted Fetal Cell Lines in Vaccines".*
October 03, 2019. New Data Shows DNA From Aborted Fetal Cell Lines in Vaccines • Children's Health Defense

U.S. FDA. (2023). *"COVID-19 vaccine safety surveillance".* FDA.gov.

West, Jim. *Pesticides and Polio*. Harvoa.org. 2002

www.FlatearthDave.com

www.nytimes.com/2020/08/29/health/coronavirus-testing.html

www.cdc.gov/nchs/data/nvss/coronavirus/alert-2-new-icd-code-introduced-for-covid-19-deaths.pdf

www.rcreader.com/commentary/masks-dont-work-covid-a-review-of-science-relevant-to-covide-19-social-policy www.Physicians For Informed Consent.org

VAERS Summary For COVID-19. Vaersanalysis.info

*"Vaxxed VS Unvaxxed"*. Children's Health Defense. www.childrenshealthdefense.org

Yehudah Roth, Jerry S Chapnik, Philip Cole. "*Feasibility of aerosol vaccination in humans"*. 2003 Mar;112(3):264-70. doi: 10.1177/000348940311200313

*"Do PCR Tests Work As Described?"* off-guardian.org/2020/06/27/covid19-pcr-tests-are-scientifically-meaningless

Zondervan NIV Study Bible. Full ref. ed. Kenneth L Baker, gen ed. Grand Rapids, MI: Zondervan 2002

All Rights Reserved
Copyright 2025
ISBN: 979-8-9859224-2-4

www.ingramcontent.com/pod-product-compliance
Lightning Source LLC
Chambersburg PA
CBHW070120100426
42744CB00010B/1880